Methods of Analysis and Detection

and Detection

Anne McCarthy

Series editor
Fred Webber

 **CAMBRIDGE**
UNIVERSITY PRESS

PUBLISHED BY THE PRESS SYNDICATE OF THE UNIVERSITY OF CAMBRIDGE

The Pitt Building, Trumpington Street, Cambridge CB2 1RP, United Kingdom

CAMBRIDGE UNIVERSITY PRESS

The Edinburgh Building, Cambridge CB2 2RU, United Kingdom

40 West 20th Street, New York, NY 10011-4211, USA

10 Stamford Road, Oakleigh, Melbourne 3166, Australia

© University of Cambridge Local Examinations Syndicate 1997

Printed in the United Kingdom at the University Press, Cambridge

A catalogue record for this book is available from the British Library

ISBN 0 521 42161 6 paperback

Designed and produced by Gecko Ltd, Bicester, Oxon

Notice to teachers

This book is one of a series produced to support individual modules within the Cambridge Modular Sciences scheme. Teachers should note that written examinations will be set on the content of each module as defined in the syllabus. This book is the author's interpretation of the module.

Acknowledgements

Cover, 5, courtesy of Glaxo Wellcome plc; 1*t*, Geoff Tompkinson/Science Photo Library; 1*b*, 35*b*, 72*b*, 78*b*, Andrew Lambert; 8*t*, Sutton Motorsport Images; 8*b*, Copyright ©BBC (BBC News and Current Affairs Stills Picture Library); 9, 14, 15, Cellmark Diagnostics; 11, Science Photo Library; 16, 20*t*, Robert Harding Picture Library; 18*t*, 47*l*, Mary Evans Picture Library; 18*b*, Science and Society Picture Library; 22, R. Francis/Action-Plus Photographic; 26, E.T. Archive; 30*l*, Courtauld Institute of Art (Lee Collection); 30*r*, Courtauld Institute of Art; 35*t*, Imperial College/Science Photo Library; 44, GECO UK/Science Photo Library; 47*r*, Ann Ronan at Image Select International; 48, courtesy of Addenbrookes Medical Photography Unit; 52, David Parker/Science Photo Library; 69, courtesy of Graseby Specac Ltd; 70, John Greim/Science Photo Library; 72*t*, Tek Image/Science Photo Library; 78*t*, James King-Holmes/Science Photo Library; 81*l*, David Kampfner/Life File; 81*r*, J.C. Revy/Science Photo Library

Contents

Separation techniques for analysis

1 describe simply and explain qualitatively: paper, thin-layer and gas/liquid chromatography in terms of adsorption and/or partition, using the terms R_f *value* and *retention time* where appropriate;

2 interpret paper and thin-layer chromatograms in terms of the identification of particular species from a mixture;

3 interpret gas/liquid chromatograms in terms of the percentage composition of a mixture;

4 demonstrate an awareness of the applications of these methods of chromatography in industry and medicine;

5 describe simply the process of electrophoresis and the effect of pH on the migration of ions;

6 describe the hydrolysis of proteins and the separation and detection of the products by electrophoresis;

7 outline simply the analysis of genes and genetic finger-printing.

Chromatography and **electrophoresis** are both methods of analysis that separate substances, but the principles involved in each are quite different.

Chromatography

You may remember with pride, in primary or lower-school science, splitting up the components of ink from fibre-tip pens or separating the colours of Smarties on filter paper *(figure 1.1)*. This simple experiment has been developed, so that we can now separate many different kinds of substances *(figure 1.2)*.

The separation of substances by slow movement through or over a separating material is

called **chromatography**. The word 'chromatography', which means 'colour writing', was first used in 1903 to describe the separation of plant pigments by percolating the solution of pigments through a column of calcium carbonate packed into a glass tube *(figure 1.3)*. Each pigment moved at a different rate and formed coloured areas in the column, which could be separated. Although many of the substances that we now separate by more developed methods are colourless, we still use the term *chromatography*.

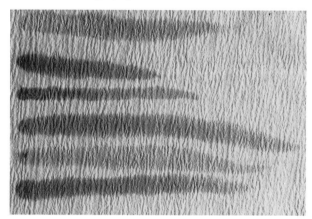

● *Figure 1.1* Some patterns obtained by paper chromatography of ink from coloured fibre-tip pens.

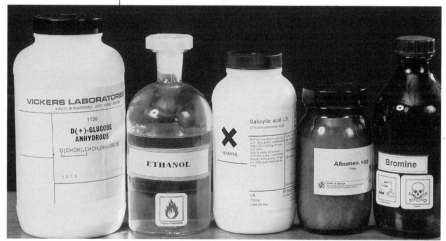

● *Figure 1.2* Examples of some of the substances that we can detect or analyse by chromatography: sugars, alcohols, organic acids, proteins and gases.

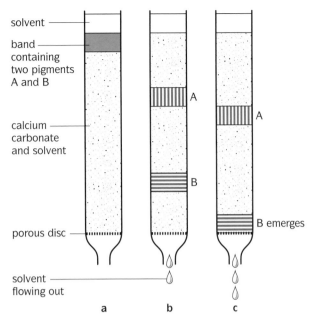

solvent

band containing two pigments A and B

calcium carbonate and solvent

porous disc

solvent flowing out

a   b   c

A

A

B

B emerges

● *Figure 1.3* The separation of pigments can be carried out by chromatography on a calcium carbonate (CaCO₃) column.

a The mixed pigments are added to the top of the column.

b The individual pigments flow downwards with the solvent at different rates.

c The pigments reach the bottom at different times and may be collected separately.

You can see in *figure 1.3* how the solution of pigments is placed on top of the column and is washed down the column with a solvent. This simple process and the more developed methods of chromatography all have the following principles in common.

■ There are two phases in the chromatography process: (1) The **stationary phase** stays in place in the pores of the paper or inside a column. If packed into a column, it usually consists of solid particles or a viscous liquid coated onto a solid surface. (2) The **mobile phase**, which is the solvent, moves over the paper or through the column and is a liquid or a gas. We call this the **eluting fluid**. 'Elute' means to wash through.

■ The separation of the mixture we want to study occurs by the interaction of the components of the mixture with the stationary phase.

■ Dissolved components are called **solutes**.

■ There are two mechanisms for the separation process: (i) partition and (ii) adsorption.

Mechanisms of chromatographic separation

Partition

To understand the term **partition**, it is helpful to examine what happens to a solute when it is added to two liquids that do not mix (i.e. immiscible liquids) but which are in contact with one another (*figure 1.4*). For example, when a solute that is soluble in both water and trichloromethane is added to a mixture of these two immiscible liquids, two liquid layers form and the solute molecules pass upwards and downwards across the interface between the liquids. When the rates of movement (up and down) of the solute molecules between the two liquids become equal, we say that *equilibrium* has been reached, and the solute molecules are distributed between the two liquids in a definite ratio. The solute has been **partitioned** between the two liquids. The ratio of the concentrations of the solutes in the two liquids is a constant value at constant temperature and is called the **partition coefficient**, given the symbol K.

In partition chromatography, during the separation process the solutes move to and fro between the stationary phase and the mobile phase (*figure 1.5a*) and are partitioned between them. Solutes in the mobile phase move forward with it as the mobile phase descends the column.

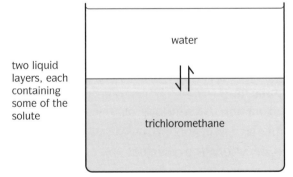

two liquid layers, each containing some of the solute

water

trichloromethane

● *Figure 1.4* A solute is partitioned between two immiscible liquids. In this example, they are water and trichloromethane. The partition coefficient at equilibrium is a constant given in this case by

$$K = \frac{(\text{concentration of the solute in water})_{\text{equilibrium}}}{(\text{concentration of the solute in trichloromethane})_{\text{equilibrium}}}$$

a Separation by partition

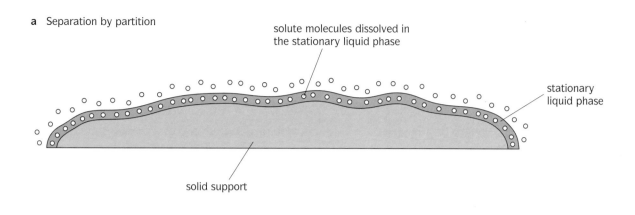

solute molecules dissolved in
the stationary liquid phase

stationary
liquid phase

solid support

b Separation by adsorption

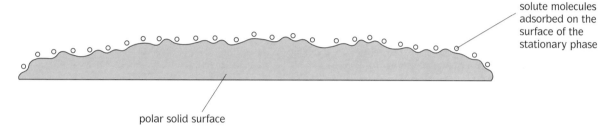

solute molecules
adsorbed on the
surface of the
stationary phase

polar solid surface

● *Figure 1.5* Two different mechanisms of separation:
a partition chromatography and **b** adsorption chromatography.

When the stationary and mobile phases are both liquids, the rate of movement of each solute depends on its *relative solubility* in the two phases; those solutes which are more soluble in the mobile phase will move faster and further than the others. When the mobile phase is a gas, the rate of movement of the solutes depends on their *volatility*.

Adsorption

In the **adsorption** process, the solute molecules are held on the surface of the stationary phase *(figure 1.5b)*. The stationary phase is a polar solid and the solutes are polar molecules (refer to *Foundation Chemistry* for the meaning of polarity). Strongly polar stationary phases attract and retain the polar solutes. The separation of the solutes depends on the *difference in their polarity*; the more polar solutes are more readily adsorbed than the less polar solutes.

Paper chromatography (partition)

In this technique we use filter paper because the cellulose fibres from which it is made contain water. This trapped water is the stationary phase and the filter paper is called the **support**. The mobile phase is the liquid solvent that moves over the paper. *Figure 1.6a* shows how the method works. The solutes are transferred from the mobile phase to the stationary phase by partition between the two liquids. Solutes in the mobile phase move forward with it.

When the solvent comes towards the end of the paper, the paper is removed from the tank and the solvent is evaporated from it. You can see coloured components of a mixture; but if there are colour-less components, you can spray the paper with chemicals so that the colourless components form coloured complex ions. For example, when sprayed with ninhydrin, amino acids show up as lilac-blue spots.

Figure 1.6a shows how the components of the mixture are identified by comparing their positions on the filter paper with those of known pure compounds. Another way is to calculate the retardation factors, which we call R_f values. The movement of any solute relative to the eluting solvent is a characteristic property of that substance known as the R_f **value**. It is defined as

$$R_f = \frac{\text{distance moved by centre of solute spot}}{\text{distance moved by front of mobile phase}}$$

The calculation of an R_f value is as shown in *figure 1.6b*.

You may have wondered what we can do if the eluting solvent does not completely separate two or more of the components. This difficulty can be overcome by rotating the paper through 90° after the initial process and repeating the separation with a different solvent, as shown in *figure 1.6c*. Separation of all the components should now occur, as it is unlikely that two or more substances would have identical R_f values in two different solvents.

Paper chromatography is a sensitive method capable of separating samples as small as $0.1\,\mu g$ ($1\,\mu g = 10^{-6}g$).

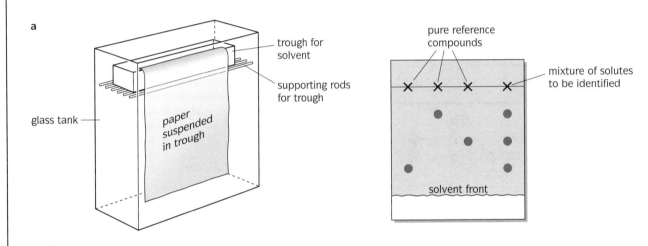

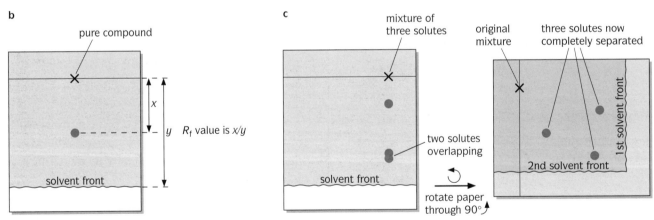

● **Figure 1.6** Amino acids can be separated by a combination of one- and two-dimensional paper chromatography.

a One-dimensional paper chromatography, showing the use of pure reference compounds for comparison with the unknown mixture.

b How R_f values are calculated.

c Two-dimensional paper chromatography is used to separate overlapping spots. The paper is rotated through 90° after the first separation, and a different solvent used for the second separation.

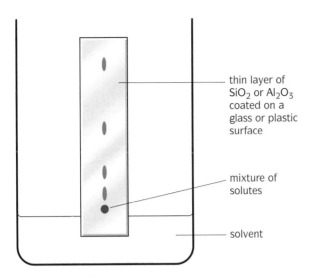

thin layer of
SiO_2 or Al_2O_3
coated on a
glass or plastic
surface

mixture of
solutes

solvent

● *Figure 1.7* Thin-layer chromatography.

Thin-layer chromatography (adsorption/partition)

In this method, the stationary phase is a thin layer of silica (SiO_2) or aluminium oxide (Al_2O_3), which is coated onto a glass or plastic surface. The mobile phase is a liquid *(figure 1.7)*. The silica and aluminium oxide are first heated to high temperatures so that all water is removed from them. In this state they act as polar solids and the solutes are transferred to them from the mobile phase by adsorption onto their surfaces. However, both these stationary phases readily attract water molecules, so that the thin layers become $SiO_2.xH_2O$ (silica gel) or $Al_2O_3.xH_2O$ (alumina). The water present then becomes the stationary phase and the solutes are separated by partition. On partially dried thin layers, both adsorption and partition may occur.

A thin layer of cellulose powder is also used as the stationary phase, but, as cellulose retains water, the separation is by partition. Once again, colourless components can be detected by adding chemicals to the plate. One procedure is to place the plate in a closed container with a few crystals of iodine. The iodine vapour accumulates on the spots of separated solutes, so that dark-brown spots appear on a yellow background. A second technique involves shining ultraviolet light on a plate that contains a fluorescent material. This glow is reduced by solutes, which will then appear as dark spots on a bright plate. The solutes are identified in the same way as for paper chromatography.

Thin-layer chromatography (TLC) is about three times faster than paper chromatography and it will work with very small samples. You may be able to try it yourself on a microscope slide. Also, because the thin layer can be made from different solids, a wide variety of mixtures can be identified by careful choice of the stationary and mobile phases. For example, a thin layer of silica will separate chlorinated insecticides, steroids and alkaloids such as morphine and opium.

We also use thin-layer chromatography to select conditions for larger-scale separations. Different combinations of stationary phases and mobile phases can be tested quickly to find the most effective method, for a particular separation.

Thin-layer chromatography is mainly used for the separation of organic compounds and has applications in clinical diagnosis, forensic testing and quality control *(figure 1.8)*.

● *Figure 1.8* Thin-layer chromatography apparatus and viewing equipment.

SAQ 1.1

State **two** advantages of thin-layer chromatography over paper chromatography.

SAQ 1.2

The results of a thin-layer chromatography separation on silica gel are shown below.

Compound	Distance travelled/cm
compound 1	1.5
compound 2	9.1
solvent	12.5

Calculate the R_f values of the compounds and comment on their values.

Examples of the use of thin-layer chromatography in forensic science are the well publicised cases of the 'Maguire Seven' and the 'Birmingham Six', men and women suspected of terrorist activities involving explosives. The Maguire family were arrested on the basis of the results of the thin-layer chromatography analysis of ether extracts of cotton-wool swabs taken from their hands and nail scrapings. The suspects were convicted. The case was re-opened years later. It became known that the TLC tests had been carried out by an 18-year-old scientific officer who had only a few weeks' experience of using TLC, but who was said to have been working under supervision. The Court of Appeal was concerned that accidental contamination of the samples from the suspects could have occurred from other materials, for example from some pharmaceutical product, and also that the inexperienced analyst might have confused samples with standards. The evidence from the TLC tests was discredited and the convictions were quashed. Because of similarities in the forensic evidence in the 'Birmingham Six' case, this was also referred to the Court of Appeal, and again the convictions were quashed.

Gas/liquid chromatography (partition)

Gas/liquid chromatography (GLC) is used to separate and identify very small samples of gases, liquids and volatile solids. In this technique, a vaporised sample is carried by an inert gas (the mobile phase) over the surface of a liquid (the stationary phase). A diagram of the apparatus and how it works is shown in *figure 1.9*. The mobile phase, which is called the **carrier gas**, flows through the column of stationary phase at a constant rate. The relatively unreactive gas nitrogen is frequently used as the carrier gas. The stationary phase is a non-volatile liquid on a solid support, for example, a long-chain alkane of high boiling point coated onto the surface of firebrick (mainly SiO_2). The components of the mixture are partitioned between the mobile and stationary phases to different extents, so that they move through the column at different rates depending on (i) their boiling points and (ii) their relative solubilities in the mobile and stationary phases.

The components leave the column after definite intervals of time, which are characteristic of each component and are monitored by a detector designed to record changes in the composition of the carrier gas as the components are separated.

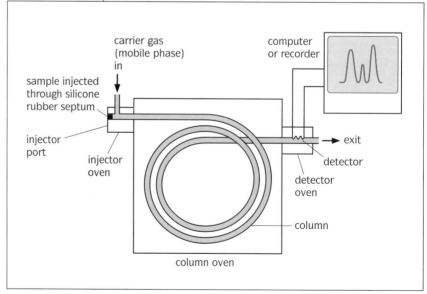

● **Figure 1.9** Diagram showing how a gas/liquid chromatograph works. The ovens are needed to keep the temperature constant.

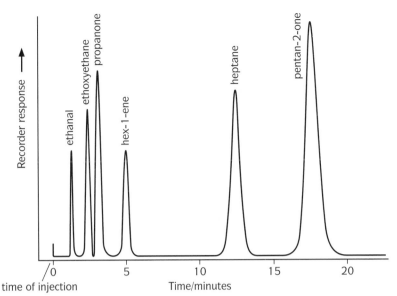

● **Figure 1.10** A gas/liquid chromatogram showing how retention time is measured. The time of injection is defined as 0 minutes. The retention time for hex-1-ene is 5 minutes and that for heptane is 12.5 minutes. The area under each peak is a measure of the amount of that compound in the mixture.

Figure 1.10 shows a diagram of a chromatogram for a mixture of liquids. The time taken for each of these components to pass through the column is found by measuring the distance between the injection of the mixture and the centre of the peak for that component. We call this value the **retention time**. Since each solute has its own retention time, we can identify an unknown compound by comparing its retention time with the retention times of known

compounds. However, remember that the conditions used in the experiments must be the same, that is:

■ the same carrier gas;
■ the same flow rate;
■ the same stationary phase;
■ the same temperature.

Another way of identifying the separated solutes as they emerge from the column is by linking the gas/liquid chromatography apparatus to a **mass spectrometer**. In *Foundation Chemistry*, you saw that the mass spectrum of a substance is like a fingerprint – the heights and distribution of the peaks will identify a substance (*figure 1.11*). The mass spectrum of each component is then recorded before the next one emerges from the column. This technique is very sensitive, and any two solutes that can be separated after *one second* on a gas/liquid chromatography column can be identified almost instantly by the mass spectrometer without first being separated and collected. This arrangement is used for analysing complex mixtures, for example for identifying the hydrocarbons in a sample of crude oil.

The gas/liquid chromatogram also tells us how much of each component is present in the mixture. The *area* under a component peak in the chromatogram is related to the *amount* of that component in the mixture. Electronic integrators have been developed that can determine peak areas with great speed.

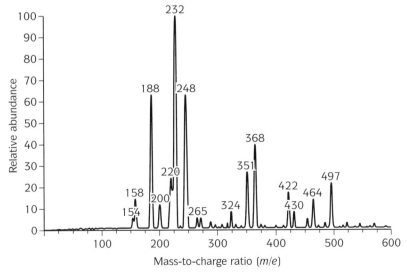

● **Figure 1.11** A typical mass spectrum obtained from a mass spectrometer linked to gas/liquid chromatography apparatus might look like this one, which is for a sample of oil from lime peel. The horizontal axis shows the mass-to-charge ratio *m/e* and the vertical axis shows the relative abundance. The numbers show the *m/e* values of the peaks.

GLC is used for testing for steroids in competing athletes and for testing the fuels used in Formula One motor racing (*figure 1.12*). An interesting example of the use of the combined technique of GLC and mass spectrometry in forensic science is the case of a husband who killed his wife while she was a patient in hospital. He poisoned her with cyanide and then had her body cremated. But the police found strands of the victim's hair on a hospital pillow and detected cyanide in the hair follicles. This led to a criminal conviction.

A modification of the GLC process uses a capillary column with a selected stationary phase. This is used in the pharmaceutical industry to confirm the absence, or very limited presence, of toxic *volatile* solvents that are used to

● *Figure 1.12* Here, a Formula One car is being refuelled during a race. Gas/liquid chromatography is used for testing the fuels. The tests look for the presence of additives and make sure that the quantities of compounds that could improve the car's performance are within allowed limits. Among the substances tested for are benzene and methylbenzene (old name, toluene).

prepare pharmaceutical products. Benzene and trichloromethane, in particular, are monitored in this way.

When we want to separate small samples of *non-volatile* substances and find out how much of each component is present, we use high-performance liquid chromatography (HPLC). This is an improved form of the original chromatography method used to separate plant pigments. It is similar to GLC except that the mobile phase is a liquid that moves under high pressure through a column containing the stationary phase. The chromatogram produced resembles a GLC chromatogram in the information it gives us. The technique is used by the UK Sports Council to detect the presence of the stimulant caffeine in competing sports-people (*figure 1.13*).

SAQ 1.3

For GLC separations explain:

a how retention time is measured;

b how the areas under the component peaks are used.

SAQ 1.4

Select a suitable chromatographic technique for the separation of each of the following mixtures:

a a solution of sugars;

b North Sea oil;

c a solution of carbohydrates of high molecular mass.

● *Figure 1.13* 'Chemistry catches up with bad sports.' Urine samples from competitors are tested for steroids and caffeine, among other substances, at the Sports Council's Drugs Control Centre.

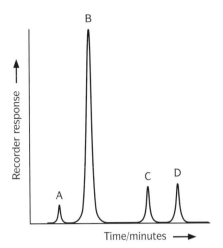

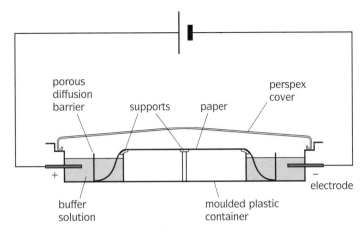

● **Figure 1.14** A gas/liquid chromatogram of the alcohols from the space above the beer in a beer can.

● **Figure 1.15** Diagram of the apparatus for paper electrophoresis. The buffer solution has a particular pH value. (If you need to revise the ideas of pH and buffers, you will find them in chapter 5 of *How Far? How Fast?*) A buffer can resist changes in pH when dilution occurs or when small amounts of acid or alkali are added.

SAQ 1.5

A gas/liquid chromatogram of the compounds found in the space above the beer in a beer can showed the presence of ethanol, butan-1-ol, methanol and 2-methylbutan-1-ol *(figure 1.14)*.

a Suggest which peak on the chromatogram was formed by each alcohol.

b Decide the relative amounts of each alcohol in the mixture.

Electrophoresis

Electrophoresis involves the movement of ions in an electric field. In **zone electrophoresis**, which is described here *(figure 1.15)*, the mixture is in solution but is supported on a solid or a gel. The supporting medium may consist of a strip of *filter paper* (cellulose) or a strip of *cellulose acetate*. A thin horizontal layer of *agar* or *polyacrylamide gel* may also be used. *Figure 1.16* shows the separated components on the supporting medium, and this is called an **electrophoretogram**. Zone electrophoresis is a simple process, which effectively separates different components according to their charge, shape and size.

■ The more highly charged the ion, the faster it moves in an electric field.

■ The larger the ion, the more slowly it moves across the supporting medium.

Also, during electrophoresis, the temperature must be controlled, as the rate of movement of the components increases with increasing temperature. In the same way as in paper chromatography, colourless components are detected by treating the surface

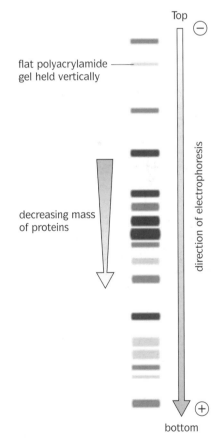

● **Figure 1.16** Electrophoretogram of proteins on polyacrylamide gel. The proteins are negatively charged. The separated proteins are made visible by staining with Coomassie Blue.

9

with chemicals or by using ultraviolet radiation. Amino acids and proteins have been extensively studied by this technique, which will work with small samples.

Effect of pH on electrophoresis

Figure 1.15 showed that a buffer solution is used to keep the pH of the medium at a constant value during electrophoresis. **Buffers** are solutions that have been made up to have a particular pH and they are capable of maintaining that pH value when small amounts of acids and bases are added to them. They actually consume the added acid or base. In electrophoresis, a buffer solution is used as the electrolyte, because the net charge on the ions being separated may depend on the pH of the medium. An amino acid contains at least one amino group ($-NH_2$), which is a base, and at least one carboxyl group ($-COOH$), which is an acid, for example aminoethanoic acid (glycine).

In aqueous solution this acid exists largely in the form

$$\overset{+}{N}H_3-CH_2-COO^-$$

This is called a **zwitterion** (meaning hybrid ion). If acid is added to this solution, the COO^- groups become protonated, i.e.

$$\overset{+}{N}H_3-CH_2-COO^- + H^+$$
$$\longrightarrow \overset{+}{N}H_3-CH_2-COOH$$

The molecules would then have a net positive charge and move towards the negative electrode (cathode) in electrophoresis. If a base is added to the solution, the $^+NH_3$ groups lose a proton, i.e.

$$\overset{+}{N}H_3-CH_2-COO^- + OH^-$$
$$\longrightarrow NH_2-CH_2-COO^- + H_2O$$

The molecules would then have a net negative charge and move to the positive electrode (anode). If pH changes occur during the separation process, the direction of movement of the amino acids could be reversed, which is why the buffer solution is so important.

Electrophoresis of proteins

It is important to understand that we have difficulty in investigating the chemical properties of proteins. This is because these properties can be very easily changed by treatment with acids, alkalis or heat.

Proteins do not have sharp characteristic melting points that could be used to determine their purity; electrophoresis is used to do this because a pure protein will produce one single band or spot on an electrophoretogram. The method can also be used to find the relative molecular mass.

The molecules that form from about 40 amino acid molecules are named **proteins**. Proteins may thus be considered to be polymers of amino acids (see *box*).

Formation of proteins

Two amino acids join together by losing a molecule of water
(R in the structure is a side-chain)

The reaction repeats several times

A protein is formed

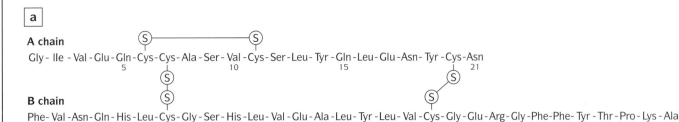

a

A chain

Gly - Ile - Val - Glu - Gln - Cys - Cys - Ala - Ser - Val - Cys - Ser - Leu - Tyr - Gln - Leu - Glu - Asn - Tyr - Cys - Asn

B chain

Phe - Val - Asn - Gln - His - Leu - Cys - Gly - Ser - His - Leu - Val - Glu - Ala - Leu - Tyr - Leu - Val - Cys - Gly - Glu - Arg - Gly - Phe - Phe - Tyr - Thr - Pro - Lys - Ala

● **Figure 1.17** **a** The arrangement of the amino acids in the protein insulin, of relative molecular mass 46 000. Disulphide bonds (–S–S–) form between the chains A and B. Hydrogen bonds are also formed between groups on the A and B chains. **b** Two chains of amino acids in sequence give the three-dimensional structure. The disulphide bonds are shown as pairs of 'spheres'.

Proteins are separated and identified by gel electrophoresis on the basis of charge, shape and size. The sample is run in a buffer solution at a pH where the proteins remain stable and charged. The gel is chosen so that it acts as a molecular sieve, i.e. proteins that are smaller than the pores of the gel move through it readily and larger proteins move to a lesser extent (*figure 1.16*).

The hydrolysis of proteins

Each protein consists of a specific number of particular amino acids arranged in a special sequence. *Figure 1.17* shows the arrangement of amino acids in insulin, which is a protein used in the treatment of diabetes. To find out which amino acids make up a protein, it is hydrolysed with concentrated hydrochloric acid at 110 °C. This breaks it down into its constituent amino acids. After neutralisation, these are separated and identified by electrophoresis.

Twenty-two different amino acids have been identified from proteins, and the proteins in all living species from bacteria to humans are constructed from these amino acids. They are the building-blocks for the complex three-dimensional structures that are responsible for numerous biological processes, for example the enzymes that catalyse certain processes in living organisms.

Electrophoresis is used for analysing cerebrospinal fluid, blood serum, gastric juices and even tears. A more developed form of the technique uses a capillary tube made of fused silica as the

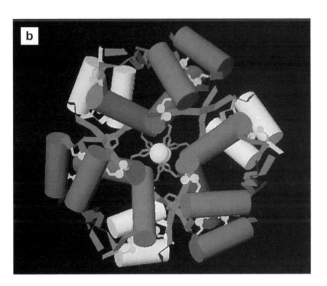

b

supporting medium. This is called **capillary electrophoresis** and it is used to separate the isomers that we call **enantiomers**. These isomers differ only in that they are mirror images of one another. Their physical properties are identical, but their effects on the body can be significantly different. For example, one enantiomer of adrenaline contracts the blood vessels more than the other, and one enantiomer of nicotine is more poisonous than the other.

SAQ 1.6

What **three** factors determine the rate of movement of molecules during electrophoresis?

SAQ 1.7

a Write down the formula for the form in which pure α–alanine

$$CH_3$$
$$|$$
$$H_2N—CH—COOH$$

would mainly exist in aqueous solution.

b How would this change if a small amount of hydrogen ions were added?

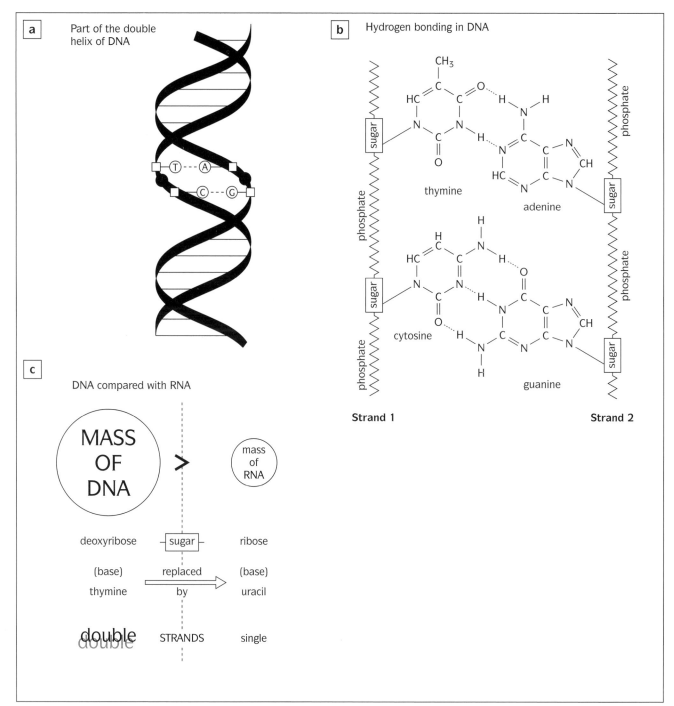

a Part of the double helix of DNA

b Hydrogen bonding in DNA

thymine

adenine

cytosine

guanine

Strand 1   **Strand 2**

c DNA compared with RNA

MASS OF DNA > mass of RNA

deoxyribose — sugar — ribose

(base) thymine — replaced by → (base) uracil

double STRANDS single

● *Figure 1.18* The structures of DNA and RNA, and the role of the bases and their pairing in DNA.

a The DNA double helix consists of two twisted strands made up of alternate sugar ☐ and phosphate ● groups. A base is attached to each sugar. The bases are adenine (A), thymine (T), guanine (G) and cytosine (C).

b Hydrogen bonding holds the double helix together. Hydrogen bonds are formed between two bases, one from each strand. The large number of hydrogen bonds are represented by the 'rungs' of the 'spiral ladder shaped' double helix.

c A comparison of DNA and RNA. The mass of RNA is less than that of DNA. The sugar in the strand is ribose, not deoxyribose. The base thymine is replaced by the base uracil (U). Usually, RNA consists of a single strand.

Electrophoresis in the analysis of genes

Genetic studies have shown that living cells carry sets of information or codes for building up proteins. These codes, which determine the sequence of amino acids in proteins, are stored in large molecules called **nucleic acids**. There are only two nucleic acids, **DNA** (deoxyribonucleic acid) *(figure 1.18)* and **RNA** (ribonucleic acid).

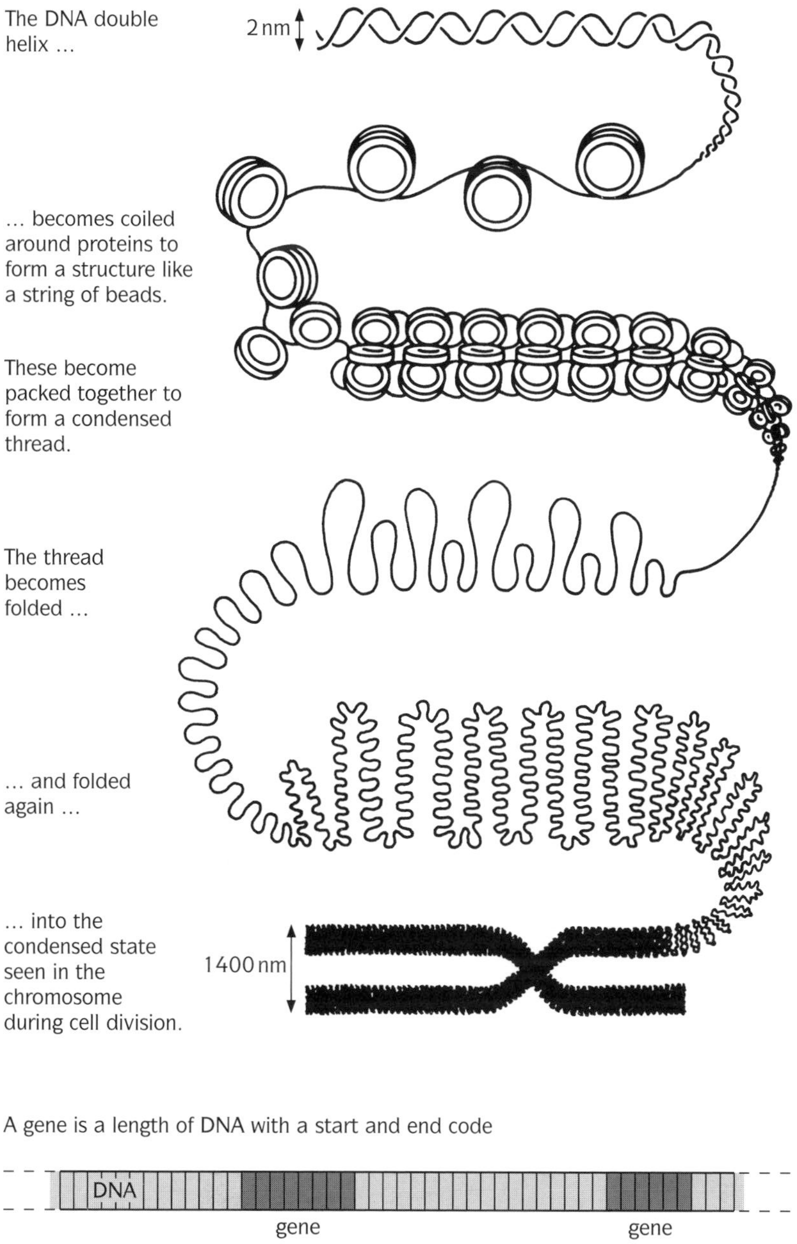

The DNA double helix ...

2 nm ↕

... becomes coiled around proteins to form a structure like a string of beads.

These become packed together to form a condensed thread.

The thread becomes folded ...

... and folded again ...

... into the condensed state seen in the chromosome during cell division.

1400 nm ↕

A gene is a length of DNA with a start and end code

DNA

gene   gene

● *Figure 1.19* The structure of a chromosome shown at different magnifications. Follow the diagram from top to bottom.

A **chromosome** is a very long chain of DNA containing a straight-line sequence of sections called **genes** *(figure 1.19)*. Genes are the units of heredity. Each gene carries a code, which may direct the synthesis of a specific protein molecule; genes are responsible for characteristics such as hair colour and height and for diseases such as cystic fibrosis.

The history of genetic fingerprinting

This genetic test was developed at the University of Leicester by Professor Alec Jeffreys in 1984. He found that there is a part of the gene that does not carry instructions for the manufacture of proteins. This 'useless' piece of DNA consists of a sequence of about 10–15 base-pairs *(figure 1.18)* and is called a **minisatellite**. He also found that minisatellite regions are repeated in different parts of a DNA strand. They exist in everyone's DNA, but the number and pattern of repeats are different for each person. Only in the case of identical twins would these be the same. We inherit half of these minisatellite regions from our mother and half from our father, and from them the genetic fingerprint is made.

The making of a genetic fingerprint

The steps followed in genetic finger-printing are outlined in *figure 1.20*. Between 20 and 100 mm^3 of DNA are required to make a genetic finger-print. This small sample may be taken from any source that contains cells, i.e. blood, hair roots, saliva or semen. The DNA is extracted from the chromosomes in the cell's nucleus. The long DNA molecules are then split into smaller fragments by treating them with **restriction enzymes**. These restriction enzymes recognise specific sequences in the DNA and cleave the strands like 'chemical scissors' at specific places.

The DNA fragments in the mixture are then separated by elec-trophoresis on a gel. The fragments are negatively charged and move towards the positive electrode. The size of a fragment determines how fast it moves, the smaller fragments moving faster and further in the electric field than the larger ones.

The separated fragments on the gel are then transferred to a nylon membrane to preserve their relative positions. Specially prepared sequences of DNA labelled with radioactive phosphorus-32 are applied to the nylon membrane, and these stick to the minisatellite sequences on the DNA fragments. To make the positions of the fragments visible, an X-ray film is placed next to the nylon membrane. The radio-active tags attached to the fragments cause fogging of the film, and this creates a pattern of bands. This is the genetic fingerprint, and it resembles a bar code found on retail goods.

DNA is extracted from the sample

restriction enzyme

DNA fragments

The DNA fragments are separated into bands by electrophoresis

The DNA band pattern (invisible to the eye) is transferred to a nylon membrane

A ^{32}P-labelled DNA probe binds to particular bands of the DNA

An X-ray film is exposed to radiation from ^{32}P-labelled probes bound to the membrane

The X-ray film is developed to reveal the positions of the bands

● *Figure 1.20* The steps in the process of genetic fingerprinting.

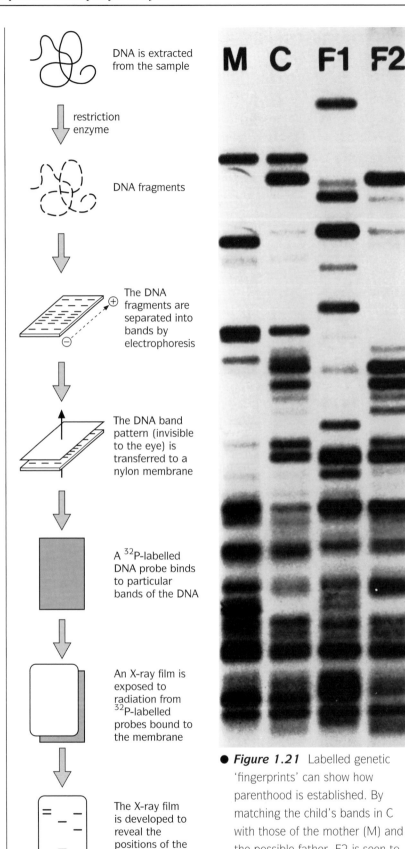

● *Figure 1.21* Labelled genetic 'fingerprints' can show how parenthood is established. By matching the child's bands in C with those of the mother (M) and the possible father, F2 is seen to be the child's real father.

Some applications of genetic fingerprinting

Establishing relationships

Figure 1.21 shows how parenthood can be established by genetic fingerprinting. Errors can arise and cast doubt on the reliability of the method. DNA decays rapidly. When this happens, some of the DNA sites that would normally be cut by the restriction enzyme may no longer be available. So, too few or too many fragments may be formed.

In small communities or small ethnic groups, where people marry among themselves, they become closely related genetically. A child may then inherit an identical DNA sequence (minisatellite) from each parent. The result is that the child's genetic fingerprint will show one dark band in place of two lighter ones.

Only identical twins would give the same fingerprint.

Forensic testing

Genetic fingerprinting is now widely used for the detection of crime. Samples as small as two drops of blood and blood stains that are two years old from the scene of the crime can be successfully used to make a 'fingerprint'. The bands produced are then compared with those on the 'fingerprint' of a sample taken from the suspect. If they match up, this is taken as evidence that they came from the same person. Wrongly suspected people can also be eliminated from the investigation.

The method is particularly useful for identifying rapists *(figure 1.22)*, but other crimes such as robbery or murder may be investigated provided some biological sample has been left by the criminal. A national DNA index is maintained using the genetic fingerprints made during the investigation of criminal cases.

Although genetic fingerprinting is very helpful in crime detection, it is not considered to be completely reliable. For example, if the sample of DNA to be tested becomes contaminated with the blue dye from denim jeans, the dye can combine with the restriction enzymes. This can cause them to cut the DNA in the wrong places and so create too few or too many fragments. Also, other contaminants may affect the charge on the fragments and consequently the position of the bands on the fingerprint.

A use in medicine

Doctors now use genetic fingerprinting in the treatment of leukaemia, which is a cancer of the bone marrow. Bone marrow makes new blood cells; if it becomes diseased, it can be removed and replaced by transplanted bone marrow from a donor. After the operation, a genetic fingerprint of the patient's blood will show the donor's bands if the operation has been successful.

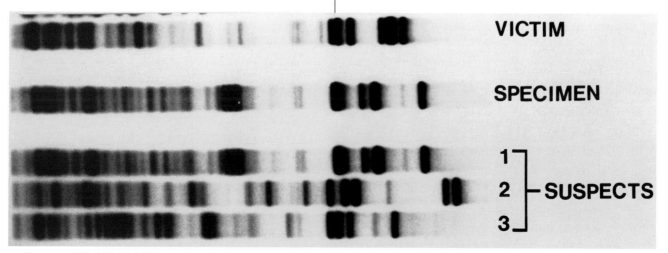

● *Figure 1.22* Labelled 'fingerprints' from the victim of rape show bands from the victim and the rapist. These are compared with blood samples from the suspects. The evidence implicates suspect 1.

A use in archaeology

Scientists are still trying to piece together the two-thousand-years-old Dead Sea Scrolls, which have become fragmented *(figure 1.23)*. This undertaking is like solving a large number of jigsaw puzzles with all the jigsaws mixed up in the same box. However, each scroll is believed to have been made from the skin of one animal, a sheep or a goat, so genetic fingerprinting can identify the fragments belonging to each scroll and speed up the reconstruction of the precious parchments.

SAQ 1.8

How and why is electrophoresis used in genetic or DNA fingerprinting?

● *Figure 1.23* Reconstruction of the Dead Sea Scrolls.

Questions

1 For the separation of mixtures of organic solutes in solution:
  a Explain how solute separation occurs by
    (i) paper chromatography,
    (ii) thin-layer chromatography.
  b Explain how the solutes could be positively identified on the chromatogram.

2 For GLC separations:
  a Explain what is meant by the terms **mobile phase** and **stationary phase**.
  b Explain how the components of a mixture are separated on the chromatography column.

3 Buffer solutions are usually used as the electrolyte in electrophoresis. Explain why this is done.

4 a List the sequence of steps in the genetic or DNA fingerprinting process.
  b Name **two** applications of genetic or DNA fingerprinting and comment on the reliability of the results.

SUMMARY

■ Chromatography and electrophoresis separate and identify substances.

■ In chromatography, the mobile phase moves the components of a mixture through or over the stationary phase. Separation occurs by the transfer of the components to the stationary phase either by partition between two liquids, by partition between a gas and a liquid or by adsorption onto a solid surface.

■ The stationary phase may be a solid or a liquid, whereas the mobile phase may be a liquid or a gas.

■ The components of the mixture are identified by their R_f values with paper and thin-layer chromatography and by their retention times with gas/liquid chromatography. Chromatography is used for the analysis of a wide variety of substances, for example hydrocarbon oils, vitamins, steroids, amino acids, peptides and sugars. It is used in the petroleum and food industries and in forensic and medical testing.

■ In zone electrophoresis, the mixture is supported on a solid gel or framework. The particles are charged and move in an applied electric field, where they separate according to their charge and the shape and size of their molecules.

■ A buffer solution is used as the electrolyte in electrophoresis. For any species, and particularly for amino acids and proteins, the net charge on the molecule depends on the pH of the medium.

■ Proteins are studied by hydrolysing them and separating and identifying the resulting amino acids by electrophoresis. Viruses, nucleic acids, drugs and body fluids such as blood serum and gastric juices are analysed by electrophoresis. Electrophoresis is used in the analysis of genes and in the production of genetic fingerprints.

■ Genetic fingerprints are used in establishing parenthood and confirming other relationships, such as identical twins. They are also used in forensic science for the detection of crime, by making 'fingerprints' from samples of body fluid or tissue taken from the scene of the crime and comparing them with the 'fingerprints' of samples taken from the suspects. Genetic fingerprinting has applications in many branches of science, among them medicine and archaeology.

Chapter two

Mass spectrometry

By the end of this chapter you should be able to:

1 understand the basic features of a mass spectrometer and how a mass spectrum is produced;

2 explain how the high-resolution mass spectrometer allows molecules of very similar relative molecular masses to be distinguished;

3 explain how the [M + 1] peak in a mass spectrum may be used to find the number of carbon atoms in an organic molecule;

4 explain how the [M + 2] and [M + 4] peaks may be used to identify halogen compounds;

5 interpret mass spectrum fragmentation patterns in order to identify the major fragment ions and molecules;

6 suggest the identity of molecules from their fragmentation patterns;

7 explain how mass spectrometry may be used in isotopic labelling to determine the position of the reaction in a molecule;

8 explain how carbon-14 dating is used to estimate the age of ancient objects;

9 use base peaks and fragmentation peaks in simple cases for elucidating structures.

Introduction

In 1909 Francis Aston established the principles on which modern mass spectrometry is based *(figure 2.1)*. He examined positive ions from neon and found that there were two types of ion present, with relative masses of 20 and 22. He had found a way of separating and identifying isotopes. Since then, the method has been developed so that it is now a most valuable tool for analysing atoms and molecules of gases, liquids and solids.

In chapter 2 of *Foundation Chemistry*, you saw how mass spectra are used to find the masses of isotopes and their relative abundances, to determine relative molecular masses and to study fragmentation patterns. In this chapter we will find out

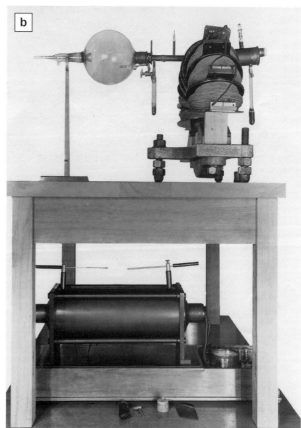

● *Figure 2.1* **a** Francis Aston (1877–1945) and **b** the first mass spectrometer, which was built by Aston.

how the mass spectrometer works and examine some of its applications in more detail.

Any substance that can be vaporised without decomposing may be analysed by **mass spectrometry**. *Figure 2.2* shows how the instrument works. Notice the vacuum pump, which removes atmospheric gases from the apparatus before the sample is injected. This is necessary because the molecules of these unwanted gases could collide with the ions and break them up further. Also the atmospheric gases would be detected by the spectrometer and would appear in the spectrum.

Processes that occur in the ionisation chamber

Atoms

The electron beam bombards the atoms and removes one electron (or occasionally two) from their outermost shells to form positive ions. For example, for neon,

$$Ne + e^- \longrightarrow Ne^+ + 2e^-$$

Molecules

The molecules are first ionised by bombardment with the energetic beam of electrons, but part of the energy is transferred to the ions produced by the collisions. This weakens their bonds and some of them break apart. We say that they **fragment**.

For example, for butanone,

$$CH_3COCH_2CH_3 + e^-$$
$$\longrightarrow [CH_3COCH_2CH_3]^+ + 2e^-$$
$$\text{this is called the}$$
$$\text{molecular ion } M^+$$

Some of the M^+ ions fragment into smaller pieces, one of which carries the charge and the other of which is neutral (carries no net charge), e.g.

$$[CH_3COCH_2CH_3]^+ \longrightarrow [CH_3COCH_2]^+ + CH_3\bullet$$

These fragments may in turn break into smaller pieces, and those fragments which carry charge are detected by the spectrometer.

Analysis of the ions

Look at *figure 2.2* and follow the progress of the singly charged positive ions through the instrument.

- They are accelerated and concentrated into a narrow beam by the electric field.
- They enter the magnetic field, which causes them to move in circular paths.
- The magnetic field is varied so that ions of differing mass-to-charge *(m/e)* ratios are deflected into the detector.
- The lightest ions are the most readily deflected and require the smallest magnetic field to 'focus' them on the detector.

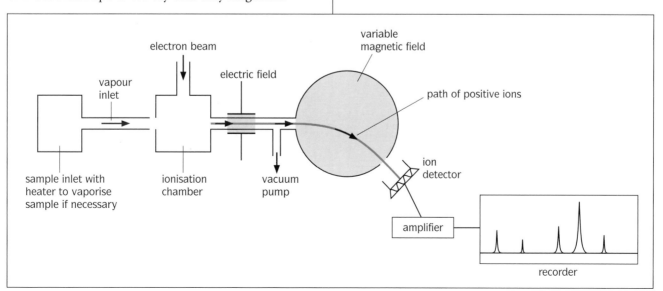

● *Figure 2.2* Diagram of a modern mass spectrometer.

- The strength of the magnetic field is gradually increased, so that ions of increasing mass are focussed successively onto the ion detector.
- When ions strike the detector, an electric current is produced, which is proportional to the number of ions striking the detector.
- For ions of a given *m/e* value, the detector current is proportional to the relative abundance of that type of ion in the sample being analysed.
- The detector currents are recorded as a series of peaks. This is the **mass spectrum**.

For the mass spectra of elements, the **natural abundance** (also called the absolute abundance) of the isotopes is plotted against their mass-to-charge (*m/e*) ratio. *Figure 2.3* shows the mass spectrum of krypton.

The mass spectra of compounds are usually recorded as line diagrams of **relative abundance** plotted against *m/e* ratio, on which only the major peaks are shown. The abundance of each fragment

ion is represented as a percentage of the most abundant (stable) fragment, which is called the **base peak**. The base peak, by convention, has a relative abundance of 100%. All the other peak heights are represented as a percentage of this. Some examples are shown later in this chapter.

The mass spectra of compounds are as unique as fingerprints. They are used in oil refineries for comparison in the analysis of complex hydrocarbon mixtures (*figure 2.4*). But remember that the conditions used in the experiments must be the same, that is:

- the same temperature;
- the same ionising voltage;
- the same instrument (or one calibrated for comparison).

Mass spectrometers are now placed in rockets to study the chemistry of outer space!

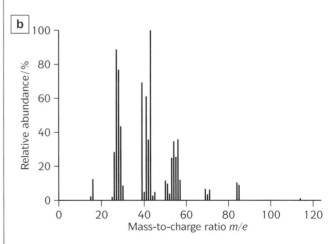

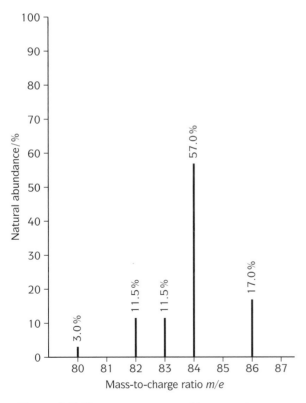

● *Figure 2.3* The mass spectrum of krypton, shown as a 'stick diagram'. Each line represents a positive ion. The position of the line along the axis shows the ion's mass-to-charge ratio and its height represents its natural abundance.

● *Figure 2.4* The analysis of a complex hydrocarbon mixture in an oil refinery may give a mass spectrum like that shown.

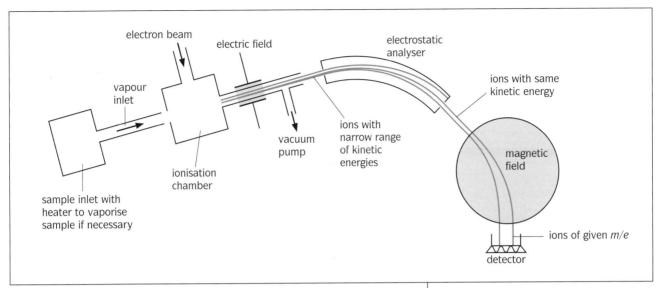

● *Figure 2.5* Diagram of a high-resolution (double-focussing) mass spectrometer. The electrostatic analyser deflects the ions. The amount by which an ion is deflected depends on the kinetic energy that it has as it comes out of the ionisation chamber. Ions within only a very narrow range of energy then go into the variable magnetic field. This is called 'double focussing'.

High-resolution (double-focussing) mass spectrometer

Many modern mass spectrometers contain an additional device known as an **electrostatic analyser** *(figure 2.5)*. This greatly increases the resolution of the instrument, so that atomic masses are determined to an accuracy of one part in 10^6.

Applications of mass spectrometry

Determination of relative atomic mass

We know that most chemical elements are mixtures of **isotopes** and that the abundances of the individual isotopes are nearly always in a constant ratio. The **relative atomic mass** of such mixtures, i.e. the A_r of any element, is defined as the ratio of the weighted average of the various relative isotopic masses present to $\frac{1}{12}$th of the mass of the carbon-12 isotope (^{12}C).

Figure 2.3 shows you that the relative isotopic masses and the isotopic abundances may be read directly from the mass spectrum. We can use such data to calculate the relative atomic mass of this sample of krypton:

$$A_r = \frac{80 \times 3.0 + 82 \times 11.5 + 83 \times 11.5 + 84 \times 57.0 + 86 \times 17.0}{100}$$

$$= 83.9$$

Determination of relative molecular mass and molecular formula

The **molecular ion** M^+ formed by the loss of one electron from the whole molecule (so there is no fragmentation) produces the peak with the *highest m/e* value in the mass spectrum. Using the high-resolution mass spectrometer, we can find very accurate masses for the M^+ ions and hence their molecular formulae. For example, the simple ions N_2^+ and CO^+ are both recorded on low-resolution mass spectra at an *m/e* value of 28 (written in short as *m/e* 28). But with the high-resolution mass spectrometer, accurate relative masses of 28.0061 and 27.9949 respectively are found, so that the two ions can be distinguished; and they can be identified by comparison with accurate values like those shown in *table 2.1*.

Tables of molecular masses accurate to several places of decimals have been compiled for comparison with unknown molecules, so that the mass spectrometer provides a quick method of determining a molecular formula. It has the added advantage that only a small amount of the substance is needed for the analysis.

SAQ 2.1 _____

The high-resolution mass spectrum of a volatile mixture showed peaks at *m/e* 42.0468 and 44.0261. Identify the components of this mixture, using the accurate relative isotopic masses in *table 2.1*.

Isotope	Relative isotopic mass
hydrogen	1.0078
carbon-12	12.0000
nitrogen-14	14.0031
oxygen-16	15.9949

● *Table 2.1*

We often need to confirm the identity of traces of toxic substances in food and water and of drugs in biological fluids. For example, mineral water bottling plants use natural spring-water, which may be contaminated with many chemicals, including herbicides and organic pesticides. Environmental protection agencies have identified over 100 compounds whose concentration must not exceed one part per billion (10^9) in bottled water. The analysis of such a low concentration of contaminants is difficult, but it can be done using mass spectrometry linked with gas/liquid chromatography.

Recently, we have seen a great deal of publicity given to the abuse of drugs in athletics. But athletics is not alone. The Horserace Forensic Testing Laboratory tests racehorses for drugs. Random tests are also carried out on greyhounds before races *(figure 2.6)*. Nowadays, most competitive sports involve drug testing. It has even been extended to bowls, and a case has been reported of an 83-year-old woman who failed the test because she had taken beta-blockers for her heart condition! As in the case of water analysis,

● *Figure 2.6* Random testing is carried out in greyhound racing. Any dog with an uncharacteristic time of half a second too fast or too slow is tested for the stimulant caffeine and other drugs.

mass spectrometry linked to gas/liquid chromatography is used for drug analysis.

Number of carbon atoms in an organic molecule using the [M + 1] peak

Look at the mass spectrum of ethanol in *figure 2.7*. Notice the small peak at *m/e* 47 next to the molecular-ion peak M$^+$ at *m/e* 46. This peak at *m/e* 47 corresponds to what we call the **[M + 1]$^+$ molecular ion**. An [M + 1] peak appears in the mass spectra of all organic compounds because some of the molecules contain the carbon-13 isotope (^{13}C),

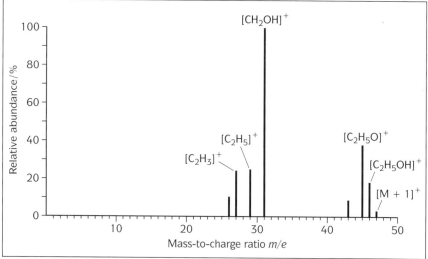

● *Figure 2.7* The mass spectrum of ethanol.

which is present with a natural abundance of 1.10% of carbon-12. If there is more than one carbon atom in the molecule, this is reflected in the height of the [M + 1] peak. For example, if the molecule contains three carbon atoms, the height of the [M + 1] peak would be approximately 3.30% of the height of the molecular-ion peak, because there is a 1.10% probability that any one of the three carbon atoms is the carbon-13 isotope.

m/e	Ion	Comment
47	$[M + 1]^+$	This has a height approximately 2.20% of the height of the M^+ peak, confirming the presence of two carbon atoms in the ethanol molecule
46	M^+	$C_2H_5OH + e^- \longrightarrow [C_2H_5OH]^+ + 2e^-$
45	$[C_2H_5O]^+$	$C_2H_5OH \longrightarrow [C_2H_5O]^+ + H\bullet$
31	$[CH_2OH]^+$	$C_2H_5OH \longrightarrow [CH_2OH]^+ + CH_3\bullet$
29	$[C_2H_5]^+$	$C_2H_5OH \longrightarrow [C_2H_5]^+ + OH\bullet$
27	$[C_2H_3]^+$	$C_2H_5OH \longrightarrow [C_2H_3]^+ + H_3O\bullet$

● *Table 2.2*

Interpretation of the mass spectrum of ethanol

We have seen that molecules fragment in the mass spectrometer owing to the impact of high-energy electrons. By identifying these fragments, we can suggest possible structures for the molecules. *Table 2.2* shows how the fragments causing the labelled peaks on the mass spectrum of ethanol (C_2H_5OH) may have been produced.

We would expect the peak of greatest *m/e* value to represent the molecular ion. However, this is not always the highest peak, owing to the fragmentation of the molecules.

SAQ 2.2 _____

Figure 2.8 represents part of the mass spectrum of an alkane.

a   Identify the molecular-ion peak and the **three** fragmentation peaks.

b   Suggest an equation for the formation of **one** of the fragments that you identified in **a**.

SAQ 2.3 _____

Suggest a reason why the mass spectrum of ethanol *(figure 2.7)* may not show a peak at *m/e* 15 even though the fragment present in greatest relative abundance was probably formed by the splitting of a CH_3 group from the molecular ion.

Identifying halogen compounds using [M + 2] and [M + 4] peaks

Before looking at the mass spectra of molecules that contain halogen isotopes, we need to know how the [M + 2] and [M + 4] peaks arise.

The only known isotopes of chlorine are chlorine-35 and chlorine-37. These isotopes combine to form three 'different' chlorine molecules, which produce peaks on the mass spectrum at relative masses of 70, 72 and 74 *(figure 2.9)*. Similarly, the element bromine, which has isotopes bromine-79 and bromine-81, would also give rise to three molecular-ion peaks. When these elements form part of other molecules, extra peaks

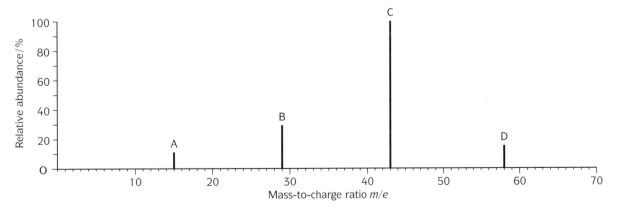

● *Figure 2.8*   The mass spectrum of an alkane – but which one?

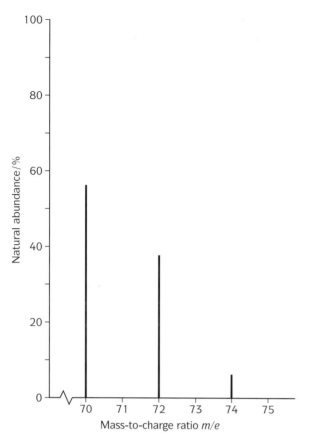

● **Figure 2.9** The mass spectrum of chlorine showing the three molecular-ion peaks.

due to the presence of the isotopes will be recorded. As an example, the mass spectrum of chlorobenzene is shown in *figure 2.10*. Interpretation of the mass spectrum of chloroben-zene is shown in *table 2.3*.

Similarly, monobrominated compounds will show $[M + 2]^+$ peaks on their spectra due to the isotopes bromine-79 and bromine-81. You should also be able to deduce that when dichloro and dibromo compounds are analysed, $[M + 4]^+$ peaks may be observed.

SAQ 2.4 _____

Using *figure 2.9*, state which combina-tions are responsible for each peak. Calculate the relative abundance of the isotopes and the relative atomic mass for this sample of chlorine.

SAQ 2.5 _____

List the *m/e* values of the peaks that you would expect to find in the mass spectrum of the molecule CH_2Br_2, assuming that no bonds were broken in the mass spec-trometer and that hydrogen has only one isotope. Give a chemical formula for the ion corresponding to each peak.

Isotopic labelling to find the position of reaction in a molecule

Chemists often need to know the detailed pathway of a chemical reaction. We call this the **mechanism** of the reaction. When the mechanism is known, we can explain why certain products are formed in chemical reactions.

Reaction mechanisms are found with the mass spectrometer using isotopic labelling. For example, if oxygen-18 replaces oxygen-16 in a reacting molecule such as water, the change in position of the atoms during the reaction may be found by examining the mass spectra of the products. When ethyl ethanoate ($CH_3COOC_2H_5$) is hydrolysed, the ester molecule could theoretically split in two ways to form an alcohol and an acid (see *box*).

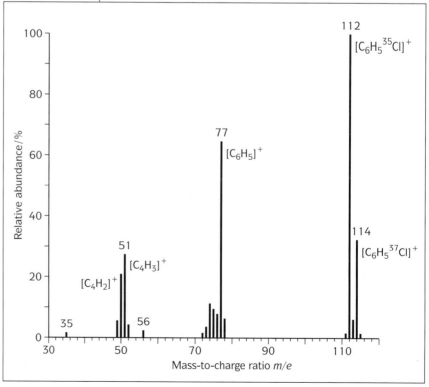

● **Figure 2.10** The mass spectrum of chlorobenzene.

m/e	Ion	Molecular ion
115	$[M + 3]^+$	This peak is approximately 6.60% of its corresponding M^+ peak, confirming that there are six carbon atoms in the molecule
114	$[M + 2]^+$	$[C_6H_5-{}^{37}Cl]^+$
113	$[M + 1]^+$	Same comment as for m/e 115
112	M^+	$[C_6H_5-{}^{35}Cl]^+$

m/e	Ion	Fragment
77	$[C_6H_5]^+$	This fragment must contain carbon and hydrogen only, because there is no $[M + 2]^+$ peak at 79 that could be attributed to chlorine-37
51	$[C_4H_3]^+$	$C_6H_5 \longrightarrow [C_4H_3]^+ + C_2H_2\bullet$ ⎫ Possible fragmentation of the benzene ring
50	$[C_4H_2]^+$	$C_6H_5 \longrightarrow [C_4H_2]^+ + C_2H_3\bullet$ ⎭

● *Table 2.3*

Hydrolysis of ethyl ethanoate

Two reaction mechanisms are possible:

mechanism I   mechanism II

$CH_3 - C \overset{||}{\underset{O}{}} \dotplus O - C_2H_5 + H_2O$ or $CH_3 - C \overset{||}{\underset{O}{}} - O \dotplus C_2H_5 + H_2O$

$\searrow$ $\swarrow$

$CH_3COOH + C_2H_5OH$

As neither the alcohol nor the acid exchange oxygen-18 directly with $H_2{}^{18}O$, the hydrolysis of the ester must take place by mechanism I. Thus the molecule that is formed is

$CH_3 - C - {}^{18}OH$
$\qquad\quad \overset{||}{\underset{O}{}}$

But *which* one actually occurs?

When water containing oxygen-18 is used, the mass spectrum of the products records the following:

■ The molecular ion for ethanol occurs at m/e 46, showing that no oxygen-18 has been taken into the ethanol molecule.

■ The molecular ion for ethanoic acid occurs at m/e 62, showing that the oxygen-18 isotope is included in this molecule.

SAQ 2.6

Figure 2.11 represents the mass spectrum of an aliphatic carboxylic acid.

a Identify the molecular-ion peak.

b List the fragments that can be identified on the spectrum and show how they may have been produced.

c Suggest a structural formula for this acid.

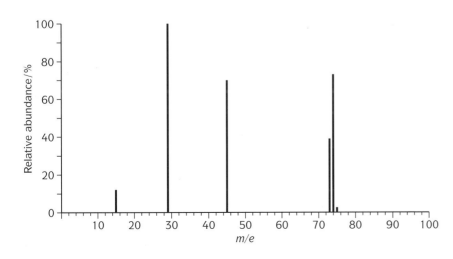

● *Figure 2.11* The mass spectrum of an aliphatic carboxylic acid – but which one?

Carbon-14 dating

Estimating the age of ancient objects is important to archaeologists and historians *(figure 2.12)*. It is done by using **carbon-14**, a radioactive isotope of carbon, which is continuously formed in the atmosphere by the action of cosmic radiation on nitrogen. In all living things the ratio of carbon-14 to carbon-12 is constant, but when a plant or animal dies the proportion of carbon-14 decreases.

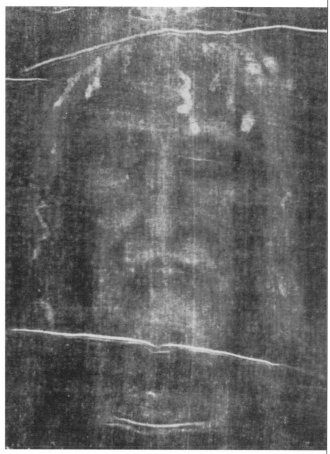

● *Figure 2.12* An ancient object, the Turin Shroud. This is a piece of linen cloth over 4 m long that shows the imprint of a face and wounds to a human body. Some Christians believe that it is the shroud in which Christ's body was wrapped after the Crucifixion. Carbon-14 dating has been used to find out how old it is. Linen is made from a plant called flax. The carbon atoms in the cloth come from the carbon dioxide taken up from the atmosphere while the flax plants were living. Scientists claim that the cloth is only about 700 years old and, if this is true, it cannot be the cloth in which Christ's body was wrapped. However, it still remains an important religious relic. There are some people who think it might be the first 'photographic' negative.

This is because the carbon-14 undergoes radioactive decay, and the dead animal or plant no longer takes in carbon-14 from the atmosphere. Since we know the rate at which carbon-14 decays, we can estimate the length of time for which an animal or plant has been dead. By finding the ratio of carbon-14 to carbon-12 in a sample of the Dead Sea Scrolls (which were written on animal skins), the age of the scrolls was determined.

Examples of how we estimate the age of ancient objects are as follows:

(a) When radioactive carbon-14 decays in a dead plant or animal, the quantity of carbon-14 present decreases. The reaction that occurs is

$$^{14}_{6}C \longrightarrow {}^{14}_{7}N + {}^{0}_{-1}e \quad \text{an electron (β-particle) is given out}$$

We describe the rate of decay of a radioactive isotope by its half-life. The **half-life** is the time required for one-half of the radioactive nuclei present in the sample to decay. Look at *figure 2.13*. The half-life of carbon-14 is 5730 years. This means that if we start with 1g of carbon-14, there will be 0.5g left after 5730 years.

(b) Given that the amount of radiation emitted (i.e. the **activity**) per gram of carbon from an archaeological specimen is approximately one-quarter of that per gram of carbon in an identical living organism, find the approximate age of the specimen.

The half-life of carbon-14 is 5730 years. To get a quarter of the activity, the specimen must have been dead for two half-lives of carbon-14. Therefore the age of the specimen is approximately 11500 years.

(c) A sample taken from the Dead Sea Scrolls was found to have a carbon-14 to carbon-12 ratio that was 20% less than that present in a living organism. Estimate the age of the scrolls by a graphical method.

Time	Activity	Log (activity)
0	100	2.00
5730	50	1.70
?	80	1.90

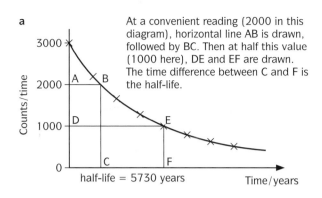

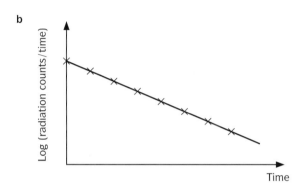

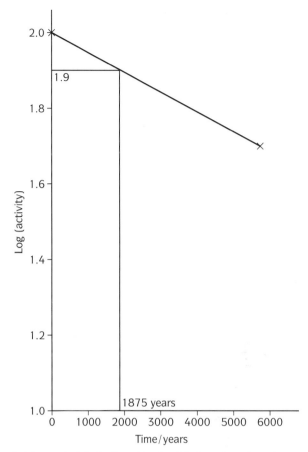

a At a convenient reading (2000 in this diagram), horizontal line AB is drawn, followed by BC. Then at half this value (1000 here), DE and EF are drawn. The time difference between C and F is the half-life.

half-life = 5730 years

- **Figure 2.13** The half-life of radioactive carbon-14. The change in concentration of carbon-14 is found by measuring the radiation emitted at intervals of time using a Geiger counter. The measurements are expressed as counts per unit of time, e.g. counts/minute or counts/hour.
  a Plot of radiation counts (called 'activity') against time.
  b The plot of log(radiation counts) against time is a straight line.

- **Figure 2.14** A plot of log(activity) against time for a sample taken from the Dead Sea Scrolls can be used to estimate how old they are.

Plot log (activity) against time *(figure 2.14)*, which gives a straight-line graph, and read off the time that corresponds to 80% activity. The result is 1875 years. A log plot must be used so that a straight-line graph may be drawn with only two points and an accurate reading obtained.

Mass spectrometry is also used in medicine in the fight against cancer. For example, hormonal steroids from patients' urine samples must be analysed, but this is difficult to do because the concentration of the steroids is low and they also degrade easily. However, these substances can be successfully identified with a mass spectrometer linked to a gas/liquid chromatography unit.

There are many more applications of mass spectrometry, but the efficiency of this powerful method of analysis is perhaps best summarised by one final example: one hundred constituents of lime juice may be separated by gas/liquid chromatography and analysed by mass spectrometry within 30 minutes using only one millionth of a gram (10^{-6}g) of the sample.

SUMMARY

- In mass spectrometry, atoms and molecules in the vapour state are bombarded with a beam of high-energy electrons. The electron beam removes usually one electron from the outermost shell of an atom to form a positive ion. The bonds in a molecule are weakened by the impact of electrons and the loss of an electron makes a molecular ion less stable, so that the molecule may fragment.

- The positive ions are accelerated and concentrated into a narrow beam by an electric field. They are then exposed to a magnetic field, where they are deflected. The angle of deflection of each ion depends on its mass-to-charge *(m/e)* ratio.

- The strength of the magnetic field is gradually increased so that ions of increasing mass are focussed successively onto an ion detector. When the ions strike the detector, an electric current is produced, the size of which is proportional to the number of ions striking the detector. The detector currents are recorded as a series of peaks, producing the mass spectrum. The position of each peak represents the mass of an ion, and the height of a peak represents the abundance of that type of ion.

- Mass spectrometry provides valuable information on the identities and the structures of chemical species. It is used to detect the presence of atoms and to determine their relative atomic masses and also to find the relative atomic masses of isotopes and their abundances. In the study of molecules, a high-resolution mass spectrometer will provide accurate relative molecular masses.

- Molecular formulae and molecular structures may also be determined by the study of mass spectra.

- Fragmentation patterns provide valuable information on the possible structure of the molecular ion.

- The [M + 1] molecular-ion peaks indicate the number of carbon atoms in a compound, and the [M + 2] and [M + 4] molecular-ion peaks are useful for identifying halogen compounds.

- Isotopic labelling is used to determine the position of a reaction in a molecule, and the age of any dead animal or plant specimen can be estimated by carbon-14 dating.

- When accurate analysis of a large number of compounds is required, a mass spectrometer is linked to a gas/liquid chromatography unit. This method has the advantage that only a very small amount of sample is needed and the time required for the analysis is relatively short.

Question

1 Discuss with suitable examples the importance of mass spectrometry as:
 a a tool for advancing scientific knowledge,
 b a technique for quick accurate analysis.

Chapter three

Spectroscopic methods of analysis

By the end of this chapter you should be able to:

1 understand that electromagnetic radiation may be described in terms of both waves and particles;

2 understand that electromagnetic radiation is quantised;

3 state the regions of the electromagnetic spectrum in which absorptions are observed for each of the branches of spectroscopy studied;

4 convert wavelength to frequency, calculate the energy of a quantum of electromagnetic radiation of given frequency and relate this to the change of energy levels;

5 explain the processes that bring about atomic absorption and emission spectra, using hydrogen as an example;

6 explain the convergent nature of atomic line spectra in terms of energy levels and use this to predict the ionisation energy of hydrogen;

7 describe the molecular processes that bring about absorptions of energy, including the role of sigma, pi and non-bonding electrons in organic compounds and d–d transitions in inorganic compounds.

Introduction

Experiments involving the interaction of electromagnetic radiation with matter have provided us with detailed knowledge of processes that occur in atoms and molecules (*figure 3.1*). However, electromagnetic radiation has many other uses. For example, X-rays, ultraviolet, visible and infrared radiation can be used to look beyond the surface of paintings, so that the materials used may be identified, the work of earlier restorers detected and deliberate forgeries exposed. *Figure 3.2* shows a fourteenth-century painting of Mary Magdalen.

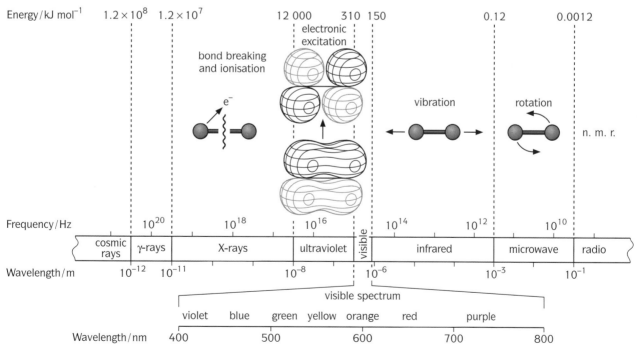

● **Figure 3.1** The electromagnetic spectrum, showing the different regions in units of wavelength, frequency and energy. These are linked to the processes that occur in atoms and molecules when different radiation is absorbed and to the various branches of spectroscopy.

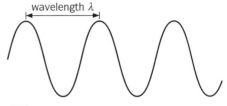
Wave representation

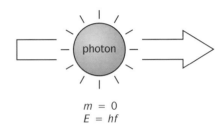
Particle representation

$$m = 0$$
$$E = hf$$

● *Figure 3.2* **a** A fourteenth-century painting of Mary Magdalen, from work in Florence by the artist Allegretto Nuzzi in 1345. **b** Its X-ray photograph. As in human X-rays, details below the surface can be observed.

● *Figure 3.3* Two ways of thinking about electromagnetic (EM) radiation are necessary in different circumstances.

a In the wave representation, we consider EM radiation as a wave with wavelength λ and frequency f.

b In the particle representation, we consider EM radiation to consist of photons. A photon is a 'particle' or packet of EM radiation having zero mass and energy hf.

Examination with X-ray radiation revealed a scroll beneath the robe of the saint that had been over-painted by another artist. At the same time, the figure had been changed to represent St Margaret. Some time later St Margaret was overpainted with the figure of Mary Magdalen again. Investigations such as these are important to art historians, who often want to date ancient paintings and identify the artists.

Electromagnetic radiation: waves and particles

It is convenient to describe electromagnetic radiation in terms of both **waves** and **particles**. Look at *figure 3.3*. This shows the 'wave' representation of electromagnetic radiation. The relation between frequency and wavelength is

$$f \lambda = c \qquad (3.1)$$

where f = frequency, λ = wavelength and c is the speed of electromagnetic radiation in a vacuum; c is a constant, i.e. $3.00 \times 10^8 \, \text{m s}^{-1}$, whatever the wavelength and frequency of the radiation.

Since c is a constant and $f = c/\lambda$, then

$$f \propto 1/\lambda$$

For example, red light has a wavelength of about 600 nm (1 nm = 10^{-9} m). The corresponding frequency is

$$\frac{3.00 \times 10^8 \, \text{m s}^{-1}}{600 \times 10^{-9} \, \text{m}} = 5.00 \times 10^{14} \, \text{s}^{-1}$$

The unit s^{-1} is also given the special name hertz, symbol Hz.

When we want to relate electromagnetic radiation to energy, it is more convenient to consider that electromagnetic radiation consists of 'particles' or packets of energy called **photons**. Each photon (also called a **quantum**) carries the energy E. The relation between energy and frequency is

$$E = hf \qquad (3.2)$$

where h is the Planck constant, i.e.

$$6.63 \times 10^{-34} \text{ Js}.$$

Since h is a constant, then

$$E \propto f$$

When *equations 3.1* and *3.2* are combined, we get

$$E = \frac{hc}{\lambda}$$

The quantum theory

The quantum theory, which was formulated between 1900 and 1915, is due to the work of Max Planck, Niels Bohr and Albert Einstein. The basis of this theory is that a substance emits or absorbs electromagnetic radiation in multiples of small amounts (quanta) of energy. The change in energy is expressed by Planck's equation:

$$E_2 - E_1 = \Delta E = hf$$

The energy is absorbed or emitted in whole-number multiples of hf, for example hf, $2hf$, $3hf$ etc, but never in fractions of hf, for example $1.4hf$ or $3.6hf$. The energy of a substance can only change from a particular value by an integral number of quanta. All types of energy exist as distinct unconnected (discrete) energy levels. Planck's equation connects the two concepts of radiation since the energy of the quantum or photon of radiation (the 'particle' concept) is calculated from the frequency of the radiation (the 'wave' concept).

For example, we can calculate by how much the energy of a molecule is increased when it absorbs ultraviolet radiation of wavelength 120 nm. The energy increase is

$$\Delta E = hf = \frac{hc}{\lambda}$$

$$= \frac{6.63 \times 10^{-34} \text{ Js} \times 3.00 \times 10^{8} \text{m s}^{-1}}{120 \times 10^{-9} \text{m}}$$

$$(1 \text{ nm} = 10^{-9} \text{m})$$

$$= 1.66 \times 10^{-18} \text{ J per molecule}$$

To convert this to kilojoules per mole, multiply by the Avogadro constant $L = 6.02 \times 10^{23} \text{ mol}^{-1}$ and divide by 1000:

$$\frac{1.66 \times 10^{-18} \text{J} \times 6.02 \times 10^{23} \text{ mol}^{-1}}{1000} = 999 \text{ kJ mol}^{-1}$$

SAQ 3.1

Blue light has a wavelength of 450 nm. What is its corresponding frequency?

SAQ 3.2

Calculate, in kilojoules per mole, the energy increase of a molecule that has absorbed infrared radiation of wavelength 200 nm.

Spectroscopy

There are two types of electromagnetic (EM) radiation spectroscopy. These are **absorption spectroscopy** and **emission spectroscopy** *(figure 3.4)*.

Absorption spectroscopy

When a beam of radiation is passed through a sample, the radiation may be absorbed by the sample. But this can only happen when the energy of the photons exactly matches the energy difference between the ground state (i.e. the lowest energy state) and one of the higher energy states of the atoms or molecules. The energy of the photons is transferred to the atoms or molecules and the beam of radiation is weakened. For example, for hydrogen,

$$\text{H} + hf \longrightarrow \text{H}^* \quad (\text{H}^* \text{ is an excited state of the atom})$$

The excited atoms or molecules give out their excess energy to the surroundings very quickly and drop back to their ground states.

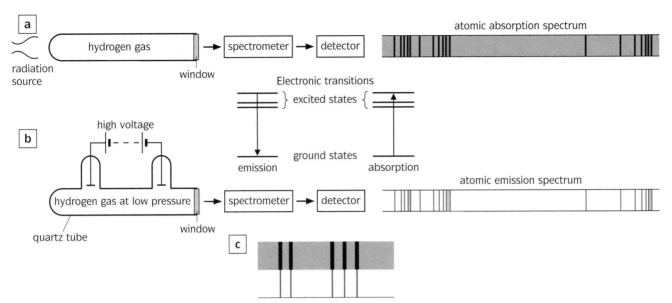

● **Figure 3.4** Diagrams showing how **a** the absorption spectrum and **b** the emission spectrum of hydrogen are obtained. **c** The lines in both spectra correspond exactly with one another.

Emission spectroscopy

When the sample itself is the source of radiation, the atoms and molecules are in an excited state. They drop from a higher to a lower state of energy and emit the excess energy as photons of radiation. The frequency of the emitted radiation corresponds to the difference in energy between the higher and lower states.

Absorption and emission techniques are concerned with the same energy level jumps. However, in absorption spectroscopy, we use a wide range of radiation, while in emission spectroscopy, visible and ultraviolet radiation are mainly used.

Atomic spectra

Atomic spectra are obtained from the gaseous atoms of elements. Atomic emission spectra have been particularly useful in determining atomic structures and in the study of electron energy levels and the Periodic Table.

In *Foundation Chemistry* you saw that in 1913 Niels Bohr proposed a new model of the atom. We find this model useful in understanding atomic spectra. It is referred to as the 'Bohr' atom. At the time of Bohr's investigations, the accepted model of the atom was a positively charged nucleus containing most of the mass of the atom surrounded by negatively charged electrons (Rutherford's model). Bohr examined the atomic emission spectrum of the simplest element, hydrogen, and as a result of his studies our concept of atomic structure was changed.

The atomic emission spectrum of hydrogen
Production of the spectrum

Look at *figure 3.4* again to see how the hydrogen spectrum is produced.

■ The electrons in the discharge tube bombard the hydrogen molecules, which dissociate into atoms.
■ The electrical discharge excites the atoms because the electrons in the atoms absorb energy.
■ The excited atoms quickly lose this energy and radiation is emitted. A pink glow is seen because some visible radiation as well as infrared and ultraviolet radiation is emitted.
■ The emitted radiation is passed through a spectrometer, where it is split into its different components to produce the spectral lines on the detector.

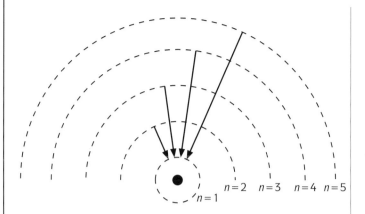

● **Figure 3.5** Electrons in an atom can exist in quantum levels $n = 1$, $n = 2$, etc. Some emission lines in a spectrum arise due to particular transitions caused by electrons falling back to $n = 1$ from higher levels.

Interpretation of the spectrum

Bohr claimed that the atomic hydrogen spectrum could only be explained by extending the current model of the atom so that electrons exist only in **orbits** of certain energy levels where they are stable (i.e. do not emit radiation). Then the spectrum is formed in the following way. Normally, the electron in the hydrogen atom would be in the lowest energy level. But when the electrical discharge is applied, the electron absorbs energy and moves further from the nucleus to an orbit of higher energy (*figure 3.5*). Having absorbed energy from the electrical discharge, the excited electron almost instantaneously drops back to an orbit of lower energy, the energy it had absorbed being re-emitted as radiation.

Each line in the spectrum is produced by photons of a single frequency and corresponds to a particular transition between energy levels. Bohr also proposed that the frequency f of the radiation emitted is related directly to the difference in energy ΔE between the levels by Planck's equation $\Delta E = hf$.

Quantum levels and series of lines in the spectrum

Look at *figure 3.6* and see how we can match up electronic energy levels with lines on the hydrogen spectrum. When the excited electron in the hydrogen atom drops from a higher energy level, say $n = 2$ or $n = 3$, to the lowest energy level, $n = 1$, the energy emitted produces a line in the ultraviolet region of the spectrum. But the electron in a hydrogen atom can drop from any higher energy level back to the $n = 1$ state. The energy and hence the frequency of the radiation emitted in each case depends on the difference in energy between the two energy levels involved. Thus a series of lines is formed in the ultraviolet region by the electrons that fall back to the $n = 1$ energy level. The production of this and other series is summarised in *table 3.1*.

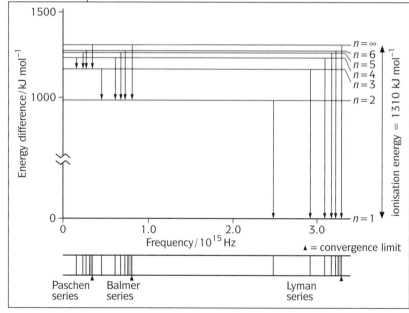

● **Figure 3.6** The energy level diagram for the hydrogen atom is linked to the atomic hydrogen spectrum. The series of lines are formed by electrons dropping from higher levels into the $n = 1$, $n = 2$, etc. level.

Lower energy level	Region of EM spectrum	Series	Frequency range/10^{15}Hz
$n = 1$	ultraviolet	Lyman	2.5 to 3.2
$n = 2$	visible	Balmer	0.45 to 0.79
$n = 3$	infrared	Paschen	0.16 to 0.31
$n = 4$	infrared	Brackett	0.074 to 0.11
$n = 5$	infrared	Pfund	0.041

● **Table 3.1**

SAQ 3.3

How does Bohr's model of the atom differ from that of Rutherford?

SAQ 3.4

Why was the spectrum of atomic hydrogen chosen for the study of atomic electronic structures?

The convergence limit and ionisation energies

Look at the series of spectral lines in the spectrum in *figure 3.6*. The successive lines in each series come closer together and converge towards a limit. Beyond this limit, the spectrum is continuous. This means that it no longer shows discrete lines, because the energy provided is very large compared with the size of the quanta at the series limit. At the convergence limit, the electron that caused the spectral line has been excited into an orbit of such high energy that it is now free of the influence of the positively charged nucleus. The atom has become ionised, i.e.

$$H(g) \longrightarrow H^+(g) + e^-$$

The **first ionisation energy** of an element is defined as the amount of energy needed to remove one electron in the ground state from each atom in a mole of atoms of an element, in the gaseous state. It is the energy required to move one electron from $n = 1$ (the ground state) to just beyond the highest energy level in the atom. So the frequency of the convergence limit for the Lyman series of hydrogen must correspond to the ionisation energy of hydrogen. This frequency is 3.30×10^{15} Hz. Using the equation $\Delta E = hf$ (the Planck constant $h = 6.63 \times 10^{-34}$ Js), we can now calculate the ionisation energy of hydrogen:

$$\begin{aligned} \Delta E &= 6.63 \times 10^{-34} \text{ Js} \times 3.30 \times 10^{15} \text{s}^{-1} \\ &= 2.19 \times 10^{-18} \text{ J} \quad \text{for one electron} \\ &\qquad\qquad\qquad\quad \text{removed from one atom} \end{aligned}$$

So for each mole of atoms
(the Avogadro constant $= 6.02 \times 10^{23}$ mol^{-1}):
$$\begin{aligned} \Delta E &= 2.19 \times 10^{-18} \text{ J} \times 6.02 \times 10^{23} \text{ mol}^{-1} \\ &= 1318 \text{ kJ mol}^{-1} \end{aligned}$$

Atomic spectra and the Periodic Table

You may have wondered how we arrived at our present form of the Periodic Table. The atomic spectra of a number of elements were studied and these were found to contain many more lines than the hydrogen spectrum. Close examination of the spectra with high-resolution spectrometers showed that all energy levels apart from the first ($n = 1$) are divided into subshells. So, in addition to the principal quantum number n (which defines the main energy level or shell), second, third and fourth quantum numbers were introduced to identify the different sublevels in which electrons may be present within the main quantum level (*figure 3.7*). From this, the number and distribution of the electrons in each atomic energy level of the atoms were found and the Periodic Table was built up (refer to *Foundation Chemistry*).

SAQ 3.5

Would the convergence limit of the Balmer series be suitable for determining the ionisation energy of hydrogen? Explain your answer.

SAQ 3.6

Calculate the energy difference between the 3p subshell and the 3s subshell in the sodium atom, given that the wavelength of the orange-coloured line in the atomic emission spectrum of sodium is 589 nm.

Molecular spectra

Molecular spectra are much more complex than atomic spectra. Usually, they are absorption spectra, and when radiation is absorbed, the total energy of the molecule is increased. In the diagram of the electromagnetic spectrum (*figure 3.1*) we saw how different wavelengths of radiation produce different energy changes in molecules. These are summarised in *table 3.2*.

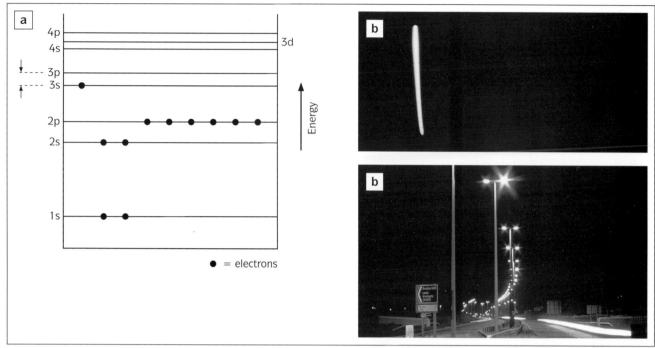

● **Figure 3.7**

a The distribution of electrons in the sodium atom in the ground state. The numbers 1, 2, 3, 4 represent the successive electron shells; and the labels s, p, d represent subshells.

b The orange-yellow line at 589 nm in the atomic emission spectrum of sodium is due to the electronic transition between the 3p and 3s subshells.

c Orange-yellow light is given off by sodium lamps.

Radiation absorbed	Resulting changes in the molecule
ultraviolet and visible	electronic structure
infrared	vibrational energy
microwave	rotational energy
radiofrequency	orientation of spinning nuclei in a magnetic field

● **Table 3.2**

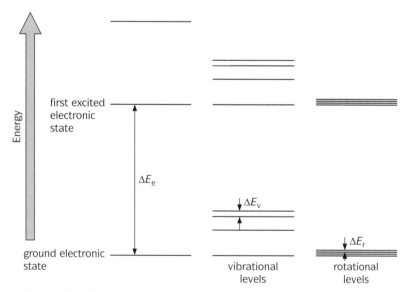

● **Figure 3.8** Electronic, vibrational and rotational energy levels. This energy level diagram shows the ground electronic state and first excited electronic state. Each of these is subdivided to show the vibrational and rotational energy levels. In atoms and molecules, the magnitudes of the various forms of energy vary considerably. Also, the differences between neighbouring levels within a particular type vary significantly.

All these energy changes are **quantised**. Their relative magnitudes are shown in *figure 3.8*, except for radiofrequency, where the differences between the levels would be very small. For the analysis of molecules, three of these absorptions are important, and they provide us with valuable techniques for characterising molecules. These are ultraviolet and visible spectroscopy, infrared spectroscopy and nuclear magnetic resonance spectroscopy.

Production of the electronic spectrum

Ultraviolet radiation from a hydrogen discharge lamp or visible radiation from a tungsten

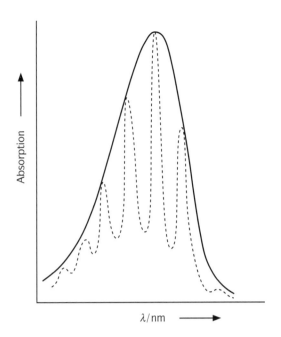

● **Figure 3.9** An electronic spectrum showing fine structure. This is the ultraviolet absorption spectrum of benzene. The broad band is due to the electronic transition. The dashed lines represent the fine structure, which is produced by the transition of electrons from the ground state to the many vibrational and rotational states that are associated with each excited electronic state.

filament lamp are passed through the sample, which is a dilute solution or a gas. The emerging radiation is analysed with a spectrometer.

The electronic spectra of molecules are called **band spectra**, although in fact the bands consist of a number of closely spaced lines *(figure 3.9)*. They appear as bands because, when there are large energy changes due to electronic transitions within the molecule, there are many simultaneous changes in vibrational and rotational energies. These closely packed lines forming the bands are called the **fine structure** and are only seen under high resolution.

Electronic energy changes: ultraviolet and visible radiation
Absorption by organic compounds

The ultraviolet and visible radiation is absorbed by the outermost electrons in organic molecules, which then move from lower to higher energy levels.

Two types of electrons are involved in this absorption: **shared electrons** directly involved in bond formation; and **unshared outer electrons** that are localised around such atoms as oxygen, nitrogen and the halogens.

To understand the processes that occur within the molecule, we must revise again our model of the structure of the atom (see *box*).

Atomic orbitals

In the previous section, you saw how Bohr's simple concept of the atom is successfully used to interpret atomic spectra. However, it does not provide us with a *full* account of the behaviour of electrons in atoms.

A theory called 'wave mechanics' based on the wave nature of the electron was developed by Erwin Schrödinger in 1926, and this theory has proved to be useful in interpreting molecular spectra. In **wave mechanics**: (i) the precise orbits of the Bohr atom are replaced by more diffuse regions called **orbitals**; (ii) an orbital is defined as the volume in space within which there is a reasonably high probability (usually taken as 90%) of the electron being located at any given instant; (iii) each orbital can accommodate a maximum of two electrons, each of opposite spin.

In *Foundation Chemistry*, you saw that there is one type of s orbital, three different p orbitals and five different d orbitals, and that these orbitals represent subshells (sublevels) within the main energy levels of principal quantum numbers 1, 2, 3, etc. Look at *figure 3.10*, which shows the outlines of the s, p and d atomic orbitals and how molecular orbitals are formed.

Molecular orbitals

In *Foundation Chemistry*, you saw that covalent bonds are formed by electrons being shared in pairs. The atomic orbitals partially overlap and so-called **molecular orbitals** are formed. This overlap creates an area of high electron density, which represents the covalent bond.

A rule of molecular orbital formation is that the number of possible molecular orbitals is equal to the number of atomic orbitals. This is because electron waves, like radiation waves, can combine *constructively* in phase or *destructively* out of phase *(figure 3.10b)*. When they combine in phase, a **bonding orbital** is formed, and when they combine out of phase, an **antibonding orbital** of higher energy is formed. In bonding orbitals, the electrons are in the region between the two nuclei and hold these two nuclei together. In antibonding orbitals, the electrons are withdrawn from this region and repulsion between the two nuclei is increased. The bonding molecular orbital that contains the two electrons from two s atomic orbitals is represented by the symbol σ (sigma), and the antibonding molecular orbital that contains no electrons is represented by σ^* (sigma star) *(figure 3.10c)*. Similarly two p orbitals may overlap to form a bonding π (pi) orbital and an anti-bonding π^* (pi star) orbital.

You can see in *figure 3.10a* that the s orbital has no preferred direction. We say that it has spherical symmetry.

However, the p and d orbitals have directions in space. We represent the lobes of the orbitals along or between certain chosen axes. The orbitals only represent the probability of finding an electron in a certain area, but, for a bond to form, the orbital symmetry must be such that their lobes can partially overlap.

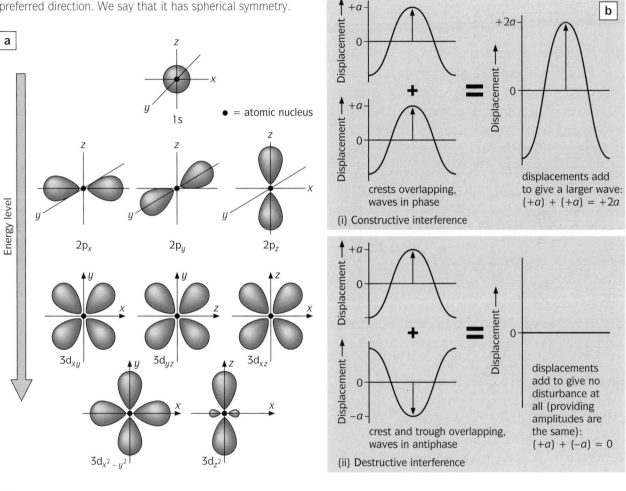

(i) Constructive interference

crests overlapping, waves in phase

displacements add to give a larger wave: $(+a) + (+a) = +2a$

(ii) Destructive interference

crest and trough overlapping, waves in antiphase

displacements add to give no disturbance at all (providing amplitudes are the same): $(+a) + (-a) = 0$

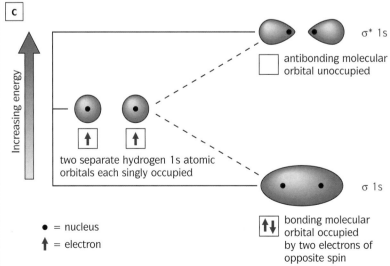

● *Figure 3.10* **a** Outline of the s, p and d orbitals. The position of the atomic nucleus relative to them and the relative energy levels of the orbitals are also indicated. **b** Combination of electron waves, showing (i) constructive interference and (ii) destructive interference. **c** The formation of sigma bonds in hydrogen.

The p orbitals can overlap in two ways. For example, look at *figure 3.11*. In (a) the two p_x orbitals overlap along the *x* axis, the electron density lies along the bond axis and a sigma bond σ_{p_x} is formed. In (b) the two p_x orbitals overlap sideways, so that there are two regions of increased electron density lying beside the sigma bond axis, and a pi bond π_{p_x} is formed. Note that the pi bond occurs only if the sigma bond is also present.

There are some combinations of atomic orbitals where overlap cannot occur. For example, in *figure 3.10* you can see that the p_x orbital cannot overlap with the p_z orbital and no bond can form between the electrons in these orbitals. The p_x and p_z orbitals are then called **non-bonding orbitals** and are given the symbol n. Non-bonding orbitals may be occupied by lone-pairs of electrons that take no part in bonding *within* the molecule.

● *Figure 3.11* **a** Two p_x orbitals may overlap in this way to form a sigma (σ) bond. **b** A different type of overlap produces a pi (π) bond. The energy of the σ_{2p_x} molecular orbital is in general lower than that of the π_{2p_x} molecular orbital, because it has a more effective overlap.

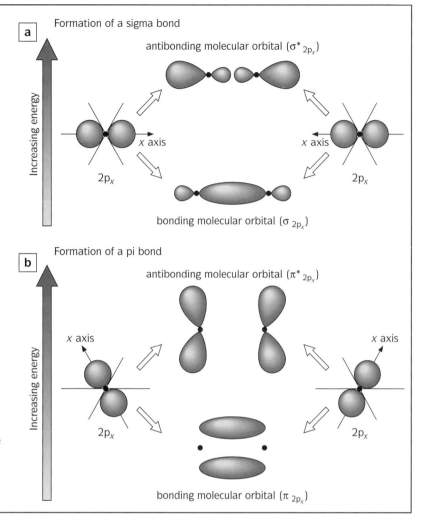

Transitions between molecular orbitals in organic compounds

Generally, in organic molecules, the bonding and non-bonding orbitals contain electrons and the antibonding orbitals are empty. When ultraviolet and visible radiation is absorbed, certain transitions between the molecular orbitals are possible. These are shown in *figure 3.12* with the relative energy levels of the orbitals. The energy difference between the $\sigma \longrightarrow \sigma^*$ orbitals is relatively large, and these transitions usually occur in the ultraviolet region of the spectrum. However, the $\pi \longrightarrow \pi^*$ and $n \longrightarrow \pi^*$ have smaller energy differences between them, and therefore may be found in the ultraviolet or visible regions.

Absorption by inorganic compounds

The spectra of inorganic molecules and ions resemble those of organic compounds (an example is shown in *figure 3.13*).

An important group of elements that give absorption spectra in the visible region are the

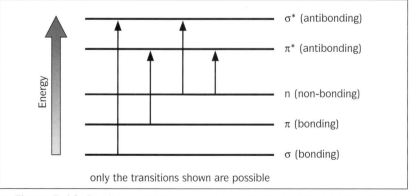

● *Figure 3.12* Possible transitions between molecular orbitals and the relative energy levels of the orbitals.

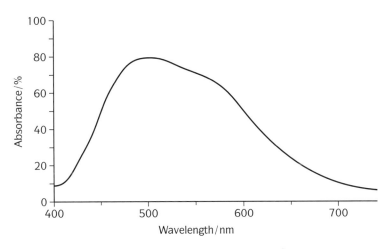

● *Figure 3.13* The absorption spectrum of $[Ti(H_2O)_6]^{3+}$ in the visible region.

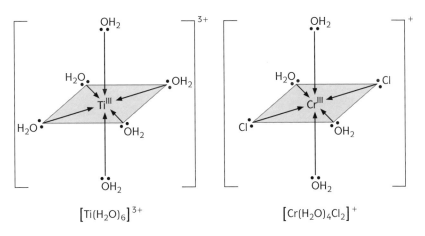

● *Figure 3.14* The formation of the octahedral complex ions $[Ti(H_2O)_6]^{3+}$ and $[Cr(H_2O)_4Cl_2]^+$. Each ligand provides two electrons from the lone-pair on the atom (either oxygen or chlorine) to form the bonds.

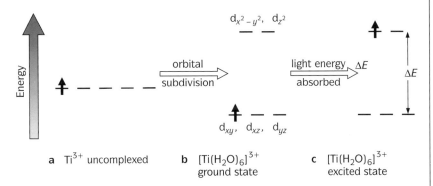

● *Figure 3.15* **a** The energy level for the electron in uncomplexed Ti^{3+}; there are five degenerate 3d orbitals. **b** In $[Ti(H_2O)_6]^{3+}$ in the ground state, two of the orbitals are at a slightly higher energy than the other three. **c** In $[Ti(H_2O)_6]^{3+}$ an electron may be promoted to an unfilled orbital of higher energy by absorption of radiation. This is called a d–d transition.

transition elements. In *Foundation Chemistry* you saw that transition elements are d-block elements that can form one or more stable ions that have incompletely filled d orbitals. The transition elements form relatively small ions of high charge density and are strongly polarising. Because of this, they can attract lone-pairs of electrons on ions or molecules and accommodate them in their empty 3d, 4s and 4p orbitals. Ions and molecules that possess lone-pairs of electrons and donate them to the transition-element ion are called **ligands**. Examples of ligands are the polar molecule water and the negative ion Cl^-. *Figure 3.14* shows how coordinate bonds (also called dative covalent bonds) are formed between the ligands and the transition-element ion, which then forms the centre of a new complex ion.

The splitting of d orbitals into two energy levels

In the isolated transition-element ion, the five d orbitals are all at the same energy level. But when the ligands approach the metal ion, they split into two energy groups. *Figure 3.15* shows how in the octahedral complex ion $[Ti(H_2O)_6]^{3+}$ two of the d orbitals are slightly higher in energy relative to the d orbital energy of the isolated ion and three are slightly lower. The group of higher energy are the $d_{x^2-y^2}$ and d_{z^2} orbitals, and the group of lower energy are the d_{xy}, d_{xz} and d_{yz} orbitals. In a tetrahedral complex ion, the d orbitals also split into two groups, but the order of the energy levels is inverted, with the d_{xy}, d_{xz} and d_{yz} orbitals being at a slightly higher energy level than the $d_{x^2-y^2}$ and d_{z^2} orbitals.

When the d orbitals are split into two energy levels, electrons may be promoted from the lower to the higher level by the absorption of radiation. This is called a **d–d transition** and this energy difference is sufficiently small that the absorbed radiation comes from the visible region of the spectrum.

SAQ 3.7

Suggest **one** reason for each of the following:

a when molecular orbitals are formed, the electrons are found in the bonding and not in the antibonding molecular orbitals;

b d–d transitions occur in complex metal ions when the 3d orbitals of the metal ion contain at least one unpaired electron.

Production of vibrational and rotational spectra

Infrared radiation from an electrically heated rod of rare-earth oxides is passed through a sample, which may be in the form of a gas, liquid, dilute solution or solid. The emerging radiation is analysed with a spectrometer. When infrared radiation is absorbed by a molecule, the vibrational energy of the molecule is increased. Band spectra are formed, which under high resolution may show fine structure due to the rotational transitions that occur at the same time as the vibrational transitions.

Vibrational transitions in molecules are related to the stretching and compressing of covalent bonds. A useful model of the bond is shown in *figure 3.16*, i.e. two different atoms of atomic mass m_1 and m_2 joined together by a spring. These atoms in the molecule vibrate and take up energy in quanta while retaining the same electronic energy levels. These quanta have frequencies in the infrared region of the electromagnetic spectrum; their energies are very much smaller than the quanta involved in electronic transitions. Molecules occupy several vibrational energy levels and many transitions can occur. Consequently, the infrared spectra of polyatomic molecules often appear complicated.

Generally, infrared spectra are used for identifying functional groups in organic molecules. The spectra also provide 'fingerprints' of compounds. This useful yet simple method of analysis is illustrated by the infrared spectrum of ethyl ethanoate (*figure 3.17*).

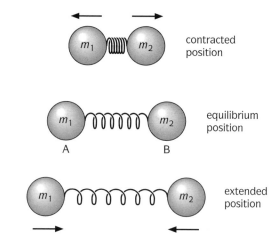

● **Figure 3.16** A model for the vibration of a diatomic molecule. The vibration of the molecule A–B is along the axis (the bond) joining the two atoms.

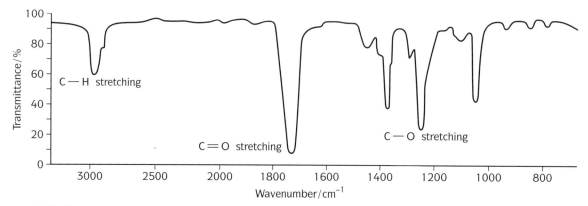

● **Figure 3.17** The infrared spectrum of ethyl ethanoate, $CH_3COOCH_2CH_3$.

Rotational energy changes: infrared and microwave radiation

Rotational transitions occur with the absorption of even smaller amounts of energy than the amounts absorbed in vibrational transitions, and so they are observed in the microwave region as well as the infrared region. The rotational motion of a diatomic molecule is shown in *figure 3.18*. The spectra are used to provide information on the mass of atoms and the distances between them.

Nuclear magnetic resonance: radiofrequency radiation

When radiofrequency radiation is absorbed by a molecule, changes occur in the orientation of spinning nuclei in a magnetic field. These nuclei undergo transitions between energy levels. The spectra formed are used for finding the structure of organic compounds. Like infrared spectra, they also provide us with molecular 'fingerprints'.

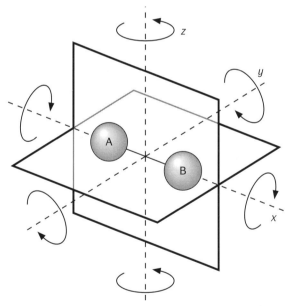

● *Figure 3.18* A model for the rotational motion in a diatomic molecule. The rotation of the molecule A–B can be considered to have three components about the three axes shown, all at right-angles to one another.

1 Describe our most recent concept of the structure of an atom and explain how molecular orbitals are formed from atomic orbitals.

2 Describe how ultraviolet and visible radiation causes electronic transitions in organic and inorganic compounds.

SUMMARY

- Spectroscopic methods of analysis depend on the interaction of electromagnetic radiation with matter. The different regions of the electromagnetic spectrum all have different frequency ranges, which have specific applications in the study of atoms and molecules.

- The quantum theory is applied to all spectroscopic methods. The basis of this theory is that a substance emits or absorbs electromagnetic radiation in multiples of small amounts (quanta) of energy.

- Atomic spectra consist of lines that are observed in the ultraviolet, visible and infrared regions. They are used in the study of electron energy levels and ionisation energies. From the detailed examination of the more complex atomic spectra, the number and distribution of the electrons in each atomic energy level can be found. This led to the modern form of the Periodic Table.

- Molecular spectra contain bands of closely spaced lines, because a molecule absorbs relatively large amounts of energy to give electronic transitions and smaller amounts of energy to cause vibrational and rotational transitions. All these energy changes are quantised.

- An atomic orbital is a volume in space within which there is 90% probability of the electron being located at any given instant.

- In organic compounds, molecular orbitals are formed when atomic orbitals overlap. This overlap produces a high electron density – a covalent bond.

- There are three types of molecular orbital: bonding, antibonding and non-bonding.

- When two atomic orbitals overlap so that the electron density lies along the bond axis, a sigma (σ) bond is formed. When they overlap sideways so that the electron density lies either side of the bond axis, a pi (π) bond is formed.

- All the molecular orbitals exist at different relative energy levels and only certain electronic transitions between these levels are possible.

- Complex ions of the transition elements absorb visible radiation, producing electronic transitions between d orbitals. The d orbitals are split into two energy levels because of the influence of the ligands attached to the transition-element ion.

- Vibrational transitions in molecules are related to the stretching and compressing of covalent bonds. They are produced by the absorption of radiation from the infrared region of the spectrum.

- Rotational energy changes occur with the absorption of only relatively small amounts of energy and are observed in the microwave and infrared regions of the spectrum.

- Nuclear magnetic resonance involves energy changes in nuclei spinning in a magnetic field. These energy changes are very small and are observed in the radiofrequency region of the spectrum.

Chapter four

Atomic spectroscopy

By the end of this chapter you should be able to:

1 outline the principles behind the use of atomic absorption spectroscopy and flame emission spectroscopy;

2 describe the preparation of a sample for atomic absorption spectroscopy;

3 describe possible sources of interference in atomic absorption spectra and flame emission spectra, and suggest possible methods for minimising these;

4 deduce the ions present in a given sample from its emission spectrum;

5 determine the concentrations of specified ions in a sample from spectral and other relevant data;

6 describe the use of flame emission spectroscopy in the quantitative determination of metal ions in biological fluids.

Introduction

In chapter 3 you saw how the emission spectrum of atomic hydrogen is produced by passing an electrical discharge through hydrogen gas at low pressure. In this chapter we will examine methods of analysing substances using the absorption and emission spectra of samples that have been vaporised and broken into atoms (i.e. **atomised**) by a flame.

Atomic spectroscopy allows us to identify and determine the concentrations of atoms in a sample irrespective of how these atoms are combined. It is limited to visible, ultraviolet and X-ray frequencies, because only these radiations have enough energy to cause electronic transitions. We will examine visible and ultraviolet methods only.

In atomic spectroscopy, the samples are atomised at temperatures between 2000 and 6000 K. All elements ionise to some extent in the flame, and the electrons of the non-ionised atoms are excited. The sample contained in the flame is a mixture of atoms, ions and electrons. The spectra of the samples are produced by atomic absorption spectroscopy or flame emission spectroscopy. *Figure 4.1* shows the spectrum of a sample of steel. The lines are sharp and well spaced. Up to 60 elements can be measured simultaneously in an entire atomic spectrum.

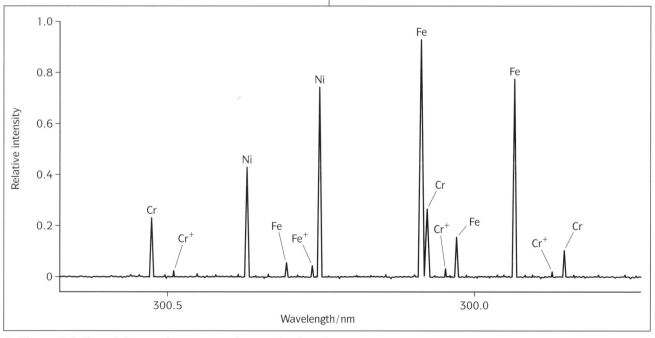

● *Figure 4.1* Part of the atomic spectrum of a sample of steel.

When metals are produced industrially, metal waste is discharged into rivers and moves via estuaries into the sea. Concern over the increase of toxic metals in the North Sea led to the analysis and comparison of metal concentrations, in suspended sediment samples, from major North Sea estuaries *(figure 4.2)*.

Metals (iron, manganese, cobalt, chromium, copper, nickel, lead and zinc) were analysed using flame atomic absorption spectroscopy. The concentrations of all but the first two metals in the sediment were similar for all the estuaries, but the concentrations of iron and manganese differed significantly. For example, for the Humber during winter the concentration of iron was 12.0 mg per gram of suspended sediment, while for the Elbe during summer it was 6.6 mg per gram of suspended sediment.

In 1985 an international conference recommended a 50% reduction of the input of toxic materials into the North Sea. This should reduce the metal concentrations in the suspended sediment, which can be monitored by atomic absorption spectroscopy.

Flame atomisation of the sample

The process is as follows:

■ A solution of the sample is drawn into the apparatus *(figure 4.3a)* and dispersed into a fine spray.

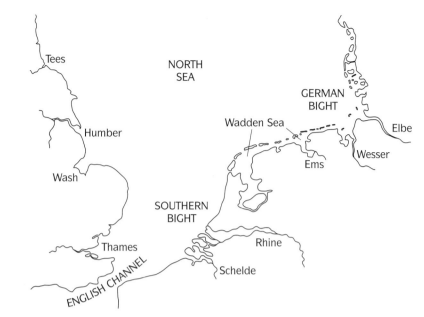

● **Figure 4.2** The North Sea and its major estuaries.

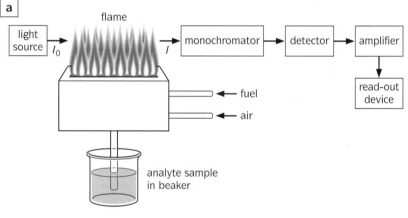

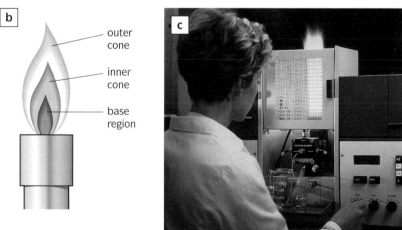

● **Figure 4.3 a** Diagram of an atomic absorption spectrometer. The monochromator selects radiation of a particular frequency. **b** The different regions of a flame. **c** An instrument for measuring both atomic absorption and emission.

- The spray is mixed with a fuel and oxidising agent, e.g. a mixture of ethyne HC≡CH(old name acetylene) and air, which carry it into the flame *(figure 4.3a)*.
- The solvent evaporates in the lowest region of the flame and finely divided solid particles are formed.
- The particles then move to the hottest part of the flame, the inner cone *(figure 4.3b)*, where (i) gaseous atoms and ions are produced and (ii) the electrons in the atoms are excited to higher energy levels.
- The atoms and ions move to the outer edge of the flame, where they may be oxidised before being dispersed into the atmosphere.

Atomic absorption spectroscopy

In this method we use a source of radiation that emits lines of the same wavelength as those used for the absorption measurements. For example, to measure the absorption of iron atoms in a flame, we use a source lamp with an iron cathode *(figure 4.4)*. The electrons in the gaseous iron atoms in the lamp are excited and return to the ground state by emitting radiation. This radiation is then absorbed by the iron atoms in the flame. For the same electronic transition, the energy of the emitted photon is the same as that of the absorbed photon. The intensities of the emitted lines are weakened by passing through the sample in the flame, and absorption peaks are recorded on the spectrum. *Figure 4.3a* shows a diagram of how the method works.

Atomic absorption spectroscopy is not used for **qualitative analysis** (i.e. finding *which* atoms are present), since complete absorption spectra are not produced. Only the element used in the source lamp can be detected. However, the technique has a wide range of applications in the **quantitative analysis** (i.e. finding *how much* of a metal is present) of metals in minerals, ores, alloys and steels. It is particularly useful for determining the concentration of metals at trace levels, i.e. 0.1 to 100 parts per million (ppm) $(0.1–100\,mg\,dm^{-3})$.

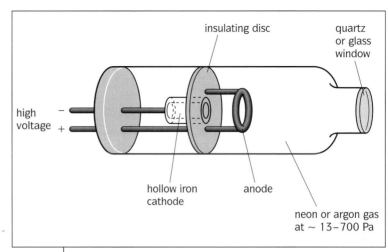

● *Figure 4.4* A hollow-cathode source lamp. Radiation from a lamp with an iron cathode is used to measure the absorption of iron atoms in the sample in the flame. High voltage is applied so that the noble gas (neon or argon) is ionised and the ions produced are accelerated to the cathode. As they strike the cathode, iron atoms are released into the gas phase. The iron atoms become excited by colliding with high-energy electrons. They emit photons of energy as they return to the ground state. This radiation emitted by the iron atoms in the lamp is absorbed by the iron atoms in the flame.

Quantitative analysis

Quantitative measurements are made by using a previously prepared calibration graph and measuring the extent of absorption of a selected frequency *(figure 4.5)*. For example, chromium in sea-water has been linked with increased incidence of dermatitis, and the water is constantly tested to check that it complies with European Union regulations.

A calibration graph is prepared from standard solutions of chromium in dilute nitric acid. The selected wavelength for absorption measurements is at 357.9 nm. The intensity I_0 of the incident radiation is decreased to I by passing it through the atomised sample:

$$\text{absorbance} = \log_{10}\left(\frac{I_0}{I}\right)$$

Under carefully controlled conditions, there is a straight-line relationship between absorbance and concentration. When metals in water are analysed, the sample is atomised in a graphite

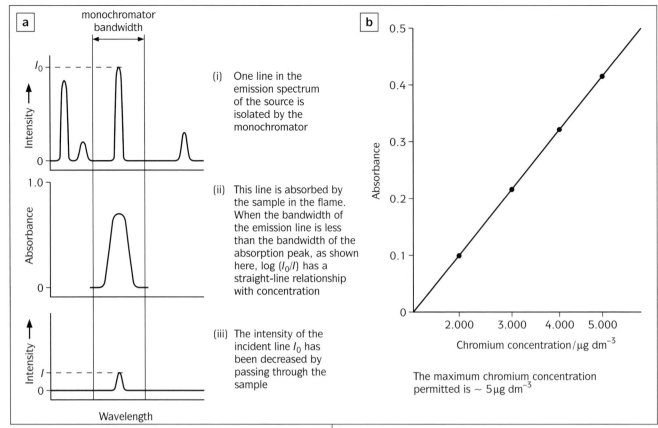

● **Figure 4.5** **a** Atomic absorption showing a selected frequency at three stages. (i) Emission line from source. (ii) Absorption line. (iii) Emission line after passing through the sample. **b** Calibration graph for chromium analysis by atomic absorption. The maximum chromium concentration in sea-water permitted by EU regulations is about 5 μg dm^{-3}.

furnace *(figure 4.6)* instead of a flame. The furnace has greater sensitivity for the lower concentrations in the water, and a smaller volume of sample may be used. Flame atomisation is used for sediment suspended in the water, where the concentrations are higher.

When the radiation is absorbed by the chromium atoms, electrons in the ground state are moved to higher energy levels. The extent of absorption is a measure of the concentration of the chromium atoms in the vapour in the ground state. The absorption at the same wavelength (357.9 nm) is measured for the sample of the sea-water, and the corresponding concentration of chromium is read directly from the calibration graph. The concentration of chromium in open ocean sea-water is usually less than 0.2 μg dm^{-3}.

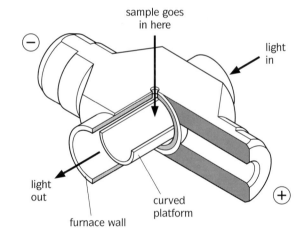

● **Figure 4.6** Diagram of a graphite furnace. This is electrically heated and used for flameless atomic spectroscopy.

Flame temperature in atomic absorption spectroscopy

You can see from *figure 4.1* that atoms and ions of the same element have quite different atomic spectra. If the flame temperature is sufficiently high, some atoms in the sample will ionise. Since it is the concentration of atoms in the ground state

● **Table 4.1**

Gas mixture	Flame temperature/K
propane/air	1900
ethyne/air	2450
hydrogen/oxygen	2800

that is being measured, this ionisation is kept to a minimum by controlling the temperature of the flame *(table 4.1)*. Fortunately, almost 100% of most elements remain in the ground state at the temperature of the ethyne/air flame. The exceptions are the alkali metals and alkaline earth metals, which ionise easily. These are analysed with a cooler flame produced by burning propane in air.

Some elements such as selenium, tellurium and lead are not volatile enough to be analysed by atomic absorption. This difficulty is overcome by reducing these elements to their more volatile hydrides, which atomise in the ethyne/air flame and produce absorption spectra. This method is used to determine the selenium content in blood. Selenium is an essential element in human metabolism, and if the concentration falls too low, disorders such as heart disease and muscular dystrophy can develop.

SAQ 4.1 _____

Some elements or their compounds are so volatile that their atomic absorption spectra may be produced from cold vapour without the need for atomisation in a flame. Name a metal that could be analysed in this way. [*Hint*: think of an unusual metal!]

SAQ 4.2 _____

Atomic absorption spectroscopy may be used to determine the copper content of bronze. State **two** advantages of this method of analysis over conventional volumetric methods (e.g. titration) or gravimetric methods (analysis by mass).

Flame emission spectroscopy

In the nineteenth century Robert Bunsen and Gustav Kirchhoff invented spectroscopic analysis, following the work of Isaac Newton and Josef von Fraunhofer. They atomised samples of elements in Bunsen's burner and analysed the radiation given off by the incandescent vapour with Kirchhoff's spectroscope *(figure 4.7)*. They discovered two new elements, rubidium and caesium, and by analysing sunlight showed that certain elements are present in the Sun. This method has been developed to give us the powerful analytical technique of flame emission spectroscopy, which is used for the qualitative and quantitative analysis of elements.

Flame emission spectroscopy is similar to atomic absorption spectroscopy, except that no external source of radiation is necessary. The apparatus is the same as that shown in *figure 4.3a*, except for the absence of the lamp. The atomised sample absorbs energy from the hot flame. Electrons move to higher energy levels and then drop back to the ground state, giving off photons of energy, which are recorded as characteristic lines on the spectrum *(figure 4.8)*. The intensity of these lines is a measure of the concentration of the atoms in the flame in the excited state.

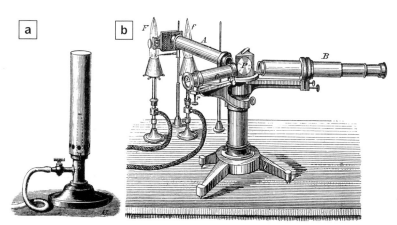

● **Figure 4.7** **a** Bunsen's original burner and **b** Kirchhoff's early prism spectroscope.

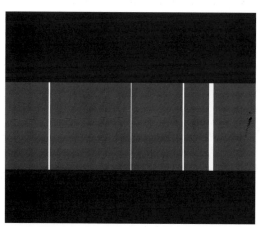

● **Figure 4.8** The atomic emission spectrum of mercury.

The 'flame test'

The flame test used in laboratories for the detection of certain metals is a simple, visual way of using emission spectra in analysis. You may be able to try it yourself. Moisten a 'nichrome' or platinum wire with concentrated hydrochloric acid (take care not to spill acid on your skin or clothes) and dip it into a powdered sample of a metal. Then place the wire in a Bunsen burner flame. A characteristic colour is seen with some metals. For example, potassium colours the flame lilac, sodium yellow/orange and calcium red.

This method of detection is restricted to metals with one or two s electrons in the outer shell, which may be promoted to higher energy levels by the heat of the gas flame. For most metals, the gas flame is not hot enough to provide the energy for an electron transition, so no characteristic colour is seen.

Flame temperature in atomic emission spectroscopy

You saw earlier that in atomic absorption spectroscopy the temperature of the flame must be controlled. In atomic emission spectroscopy, flame control is even more important, because the intensities of the emitted spectral lines are more sensitive to temperature variation than are the atomic absorption lines. For example, with a 2450 K flame, the number of sodium atoms in the excited 3p state is increased by about 3% by a 10 K rise in temperature, and the intensity of the emission also increases by about 3%.

Qualitative analysis

Flame emission spectroscopy is used for qualitative analysis. Complete spectra are recorded and the elements present are identified by the wavelengths of the lines, which are unique to each element. Comparisons are made with previously recorded spectra from known elements.

Quantitative analysis

The technique is also useful for quantitative analysis and the method is similar to that used in atomic absorption spectroscopy. An emission line for the element to be analysed is selected and a calibration graph is used to find the relationship between the intensity of that line and the concentration of the element. An important application of flame emission spectroscopy is in clinical diagnosis. The concentrations of sodium and potassium in blood serum and other biological samples are frequently required. Instrument manufacturers have designed a simplified spectrometer for the analysis of lithium, sodium and potassium, which is called a **flame photometer** *(figure 4.9)*.

In this instrument, a low-temperature flame is used to prevent the excitation of other metals. The resulting spectra are simple, and the required emission lines are isolated using filters.

The use of an 'internal standard'

An **internal standard** is a substance different from the sample to be analysed, which is added to the sample to form a mixture. The mixture is analysed and a signal from the sample is compared with one from the internal standard. Lithium is used as an internal standard in the analysis of sodium and potassium. (Lithium must *not* be present in the original sample, otherwise the method is inaccurate).

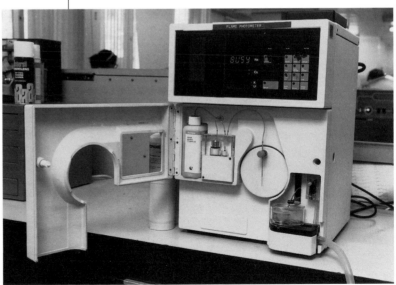

● *Figure 4.9* A flame photometer.

- A known amount of pure lithium is added to each standard solution and to the sample.
- The ratio of the intensity of a selected line from the sample to the intensity of a selected line from lithium is used to determine the sample concentration.

The internal standard method gives more accurate results because the intensities of the sample line and the lithium line are affected to the same extent by flame temperature and background radiation.

SAQ 4.3

Flame temperature is important in both atomic absorption spectroscopy and flame emission spectroscopy. In which technique is it the more crucial, and why?

SAQ 4.4

Atomic absorption spectroscopy is a reliable technique for the determination of trace levels of metals. Why is a flame photometer preferred for the analysis of sodium and potassium?

Interference in atomic spectroscopy measurements

Any effect that changes the intensity of a spectral line from a sample while its concentration remains unchanged is called **interference**. There are three types of interference: spectral, chemical and ionisation. Many different methods are used to reduce or eliminate their effects.

Spectral interference

Spectral interference occurs when the signal from the line being measured overlaps with signals from other elements. This can be avoided by careful selection of the line to be analysed. Spectral interference in the form of background radiation also arises from unwanted signals from other elements or molecules in the flame or from particles scattering radiation.

In flame emission spectroscopy, we can find a correction for background radiation by averaging measurements close to the selected line.

In flame absorption spectroscopy, we find the background correction by passing radiation from a deuterium lamp through the flame, alternating with radiation from the lamp source. Radiation from the deuterium lamp is absorbed and scattered by the background only. On the other hand, radiation from the lamp source is absorbed by the sample *and* absorbed and scattered by the background. The difference between the absorption measured with the lamp source on the selected line and the absorption measured with the deuterium lamp gives the corrected absorption.

Chemical interference

Chemical interference occurs when some component of the sample decreases the extent of atomisation. This reduces the concentration of the atoms in the flame and leads to low results. For example, the presence of sulphate and phosphate decreases the absorbance of calcium because they form non-volatile compounds with calcium. This effect can be reduced or eliminated in two ways: by using higher flame temperatures, or by adding other chemical species to the flame that act as releasing or protective agents.

- **Releasing agents** are cations that react selectively with anions that interfere with the analysis. For example, the releasing agent strontium is added in the analysis of calcium because it forms non-volatile strontium phosphate.
- **Protective agents** preferentially form stable volatile complexes with the species being analysed. For example, edta is added in the analysis of calcium. It forms a volatile complex with calcium and prevents the formation of calcium sulphate and calcium phosphate.

Ionisation interference

You saw earlier that, when the concentration of neutral atoms is being determined, ionisation must be minimised. This is done when possible by controlling the temperature of the flame. However, in the analysis of alkali metals and other elements at higher temperatures, it may be necessary to use an ionisation suppressor. An ionisation suppressor is an element that is added to decrease the ionisation of the species being analysed by producing a high concentration of electrons in the flame. For example, caesium chloride is added in the analysis of potassium. Caesium ionises more easily than potassium and produces a high concentration of electrons, which suppresses the ionisation of potassium:

$$Cs \longrightarrow Cs^+ + e^- \quad \text{and} \quad K^+ + e^- \longrightarrow K$$

Flame emission spectroscopy and flame atomic absorption spectroscopy complement one another. The flame emission method works for elements that are easily ionised, while the atomic absorption method needs minimum ionisation. They are both used for determining the concentration of metals at trace levels. The accuracy of the results in each case is 1 to 4% for flame emission spectroscopy and 0.5 to 2% for atomic absorption spectroscopy.

Questions

1 Compare the advantages and disadvantages of atomic absorption spectroscopy and flame emission spectroscopy in the analysis of metals.

2 0.20 g of nickel steel was dissolved in nitric acid and diluted to 1 dm³. This solution and five standard solutions were analysed for nickel by atomic absorption spectroscopy. The results were as follows (1 ppm = 1 mg dm⁻³):

Nickel concentration/ppm	Absorbance
2	0.150
4	0.282
6	0.407
8	0.532
10	0.655
sample	0.350

Calculate the percentage of nickel in the steel. [*Hint*: use a graphical method.]

SUMMARY

- In atomic spectroscopy, samples in solution are atomised in a flame. Electrons in the atoms become excited, and some ions form in the flame. Absorption and emission of visible and ultraviolet radiation from the gaseous atoms are measured.

- The fuel and oxidising agent are chosen to determine the temperature of the flame. They affect the extent of interference that may arise with absorption and emission measurements.

- In atomic absorption spectroscopy, a hollow-cathode lamp is the source radiation. This contains a vapour of the same element as that being analysed. The atoms in the vapour are excited and return to the ground state by emitting radiation at certain frequencies. The atoms of the sample in the flame absorb this radiation at the same frequencies, and electrons in these atoms move from the ground state to higher energy levels. The extent of absorption is a measure of the concentration of the atoms in the flame in the ground state.

- Ionisation must be kept to a minimum, and for some elements this can be done by controlling the temperature of the flame. Elements that are not sufficiently volatile are converted into their more volatile hydrides.

- Atomic absorption spectroscopy is not useful for qualitative analysis, because complete spectra are not produced. It is, however, a valuable tool for quantitative analysis. A calibration graph is prepared from standard solutions using a selected absorption frequency. The absorption of the same frequency by the sample is measured and the corresponding concentration is read from the calibration graph.

- In flame emission spectroscopy, no external source of radiation is necessary. The atomised sample absorbs energy from the hot flame. Electrons move to higher energy levels and then drop back to the ground state, giving off photons of energy, which are recorded as characteristic lines on the spectrum.

- The intensity of these lines is altered by relatively small temperature changes, so the temperature of the flame must be controlled. Flame emission spectra are much more sensitive to flame temperature variation than are atomic absorption spectra.

- Flame emission spectroscopy is used for qualitative analysis, since complete spectra are recorded. The technique is also used for quantitative analysis and, as in atomic absorption, a calibration graph is used to find the relationship between the intensity of a selected line and the concentration of the element.

- Flame emission spectroscopy is particularly useful for the analysis of sodium and potassium in blood serum and other biological samples. A simplified instrument called a flame photometer is used for the routine analysis of these elements. A low-temperature flame is used and lithium may be added as an internal standard.

- In both atomic absorption spectroscopy and flame emission spectroscopy, the signal from the line being measured must not overlap with that of another element. Also the measurements must be corrected for background radiation.

- Chemical interference is reduced by adding releasing agents, which remove interfering species by forming non-volatile compounds with them. Protective agents are also used, which preferentially form volatile complexes with the elements being analysed.

- Ionisation interference is reduced by adding elements such as caesium that ionise easily and provide a high concentration of electrons, which suppresses the ionisation of the sample element.

Chapter five

Ultraviolet and visible spectroscopy, including colorimetry

By the end of this chapter you should be able to:

1 explain how simple molecules and ions (NH_3, H_2O and Cl^-) act as ligands;

2 explain the role of d orbitals in producing colour in transition-element complexes;

3 predict the colour of a complex from its visible spectrum;

4 explain the lack of colour in Zn^{2+}, Pb^{2+} and Cu^+ complexes and in compounds containing the Ti^{4+} ion;

5 explain qualitatively the effects of different ligands on the stereochemistry and hence explain the absorption and colour of given complexes, e.g. Co^{2+} with H_2O and Cl^-;

6 identify the electronic transitions responsible for absorption in organic molecules and predict whether a molecule will absorb in the visible region;

7 explain in qualitative terms the effects of delocalisation on absorption in the visible region;

8 explain the colour changes in acid–base indicators (methyl orange and phenolphthalein) in terms of a change in the chromophores;

9 describe the essential features of a colorimeter;

10 choose suitable wavelengths (or filters) for absorbance experiments;

11 use Beer's law to calculate the concentration of a given species in solution, and to determine the path length used in a given colorimeter;

12 describe how to determine concentrations of complexes by calibration with known solutions (e.g. Cu in an alloy and Fe^{3+} using thiocyanate);

13 calculate the stoichiometry of a complex ion from given relevant data.

Introduction

In this chapter we will explore how changes in the electronic structure of ions and molecules caused by the absorption of ultraviolet and visible radiation may be used in analysis. Look again at *figures 3.9* and *3.13*. These show ultraviolet and visible absorption bands caused by certain chemical species. The identity of an unknown substance could be found by comparing its absorption bands with those of known substances. In general, the inferences made would have to be confirmed by other techniques, such as mass spectrometry and nuclear magnetic resonance. In contrast to this, ultraviolet and visible spectroscopy is one of the most useful tools for *quantitative analysis*, and more than 90% of clinical analyses are based on this technique *(figure 5.1)*. For example, the formation of haemoglobin and other substances in the

● *Figure 5.1* In a pathology laboratory, most of the clinical analyses are based on the technique of ultraviolet/visible spectroscopy.

Increase of iron in serum	Decrease of iron in serum
acute liver disease	malignancy
lead poisoning	rheumatoid arthritis
pernicious anaemia	chronic renal disease

● *Table 5.1*

human body is dependent on the presence of iron. Iron is absorbed into the bloodstream from the small intestine and carried to the bone marrow, where it is attached to a protein called *transferrin*. All the iron available for biosynthesis is transported around the body in the Fe^{3+} state attached to transferrin. Human blood consists of approximately 45% cells (by volume) and 55% liquid. When whole blood is sampled without an anti-coagulant, the cells clot and can be removed. The remaining liquid is called **blood serum**. Measurement of the relatively small amounts of iron in the serum is helpful in diagnosing some disorders. *Table 5.1* shows that certain diseases may cause the iron content of serum to increase or decrease.

Iron concentration in blood serum is normally about 1×10^{-6} g cm^{-3} attached to transferrin.

The iron ions in the serum are treated with a reagent called *ferrozine*, which forms a purple complex with them. The extent of absorption of visible radiation by this complex is used to measure the concentration of iron in blood serum.

Transition-element complexes

In chapter 3 you saw that a **ligand** is a polar molecule or a negative ion with a lone-pair of electrons and that transition-element ions have a high charge density and are strongly polarising.

Figure 5.2 shows that ammonia, water and the chloride ion can act as ligands. The transition-element ions attract the negative part of the ligands and form coordinate bonds (dative covalent bonds) with them by accepting electron-pairs into their empty (vacant) 3d, 4s and 4p orbitals. (The orbital shapes and symmetries are shown in *figure 3.10*.)

Since the water molecule acts as a ligand, transition-element ions are hydrated in aqueous solution, e.g. $[Cu(H_2O)_6]^{2+}$, hexaaquacopper(II) ion. Ammonia forms complexes such as $[Cr(NH_3)_6]^{3+}$, hexaamminechromium(III) ion; and chloride ions form complexes such as $[CoCl_4]^{2-}$, tetrachloro-cobalt(II) ion.

When the ligand is a neutral molecule, the whole complex carries the charge of the metal ion and is called a **cationic complex**, e.g. $[Cu(H_2O)_6]^{2+}$. When the ligand carries a sufficiently large negative charge, the overall charge on the complex may be negative, e.g. the anionic complex $[CoCl_4]^{2-}$.

The number and positions of the ligands arranged around the metal ion also give the complex ion a particular shape. Look at *figure 5.3*. $[Cu(H_2O)_6]^{2+}$ and $[Cr(NH_3)_6]^{3+}$ are octahedral in shape, and $[CoCl_4]^{2-}$ is tetrahedral.

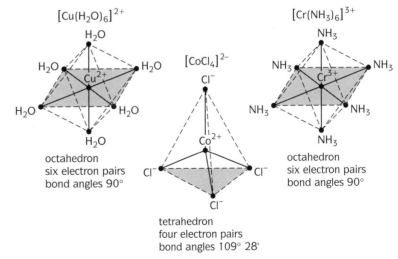

● **Figure 5.2** Chemical structures of NH_3, H_2O and Cl^- showing the lone-pairs of electrons.

● **Figure 5.3** Octahedral and tetrahedral structures are found in transition-element ions.

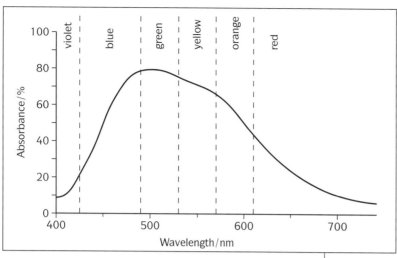

● **Figure 5.4** The absorption spectrum of $[Ti(H_2O)_6]^{3+}$ in the visible region showing which colours are absorbed.

Colour in transition-element complexes

Look again at chapter 3 and see how the five d orbitals of a transition-element ion are split into two energy groups by the presence of the ligands. The complex ion $[Ti(H_2O)_6]^{3+}$ has only one d electron in the lower energy level. When radiation in the visible region is absorbed by the complex ion, this electron will move to the higher energy level, i.e. a **d–d transition** occurs. The energy difference between the lower and upper energy levels is found by using Planck's equation $\Delta E = hf$.

The aqueous solution of $[Ti(H_2O)_6]^{3+}$ is purple. To understand why this is so, look at *figure 5.4*.

Wavelength absorbed/nm	Colour observed (transmitted)
400 (violet)	yellow-green
425 (dark blue)	yellow
450 (blue)	orange
490 (blue-green)	red
510 (green)	purple
530 (yellow-green)	violet
550 (yellow)	dark blue
590 (orange)	blue
640 (red)	blue-green
730 (purple)	green

● **Table 5.2** Relationship between wavelength absorbed and colour observed (complementary colour)

The solution of $[Ti(H_2O)_6]^{3+}$ absorbs the blue, green, yellow and orange parts of the visible spectrum, leaving only the violet and red parts, which give it a purple colour.

In transition-element complexes:

■ The radiation *absorbed* corresponds to the frequencies of the d–d transitions.

■ The colours that we see are determined by the wavelengths that are not absorbed by the complexes (*table 5.2*).

Why some metal ions and compounds lack colour

There are two conditions for a d–d electronic transition to occur between the lower and upper energy levels. There must be:

■ at least one electron in the lower level that can be promoted to the higher level;

■ at least one half-filled orbital (vacancy) in the upper level to accept the electron.

This means that the d orbitals must contain at least one **unpaired electron**.

Look at the electronic configurations in *table 5.3* to understand the following examples. Sc^{3+} and Ti^{4+} have no d electrons in the lower level. Zn^{2+}, Pb^{2+} and Cu^+ have no vacancy in the upper level, as each of them has ten d electrons. Hence, none of these species is coloured.

How changing the ligand alters the colour of the complex ion

The size of the energy difference ΔE between the d orbitals in the upper and lower levels in a complex ion determines its colour. If ΔE is altered, the frequency of the radiation absorbed to bring about the d–d transition is changed. This means that the frequency of the transmitted radiation also changes and consequently so does the colour seen.

ΔE may be altered by exchanging one ligand for another and by changing the shape of the complex ion.

Element	Atomic number	Electronic arrangement of the atom	Ion	Electronic arrangement of the ion
scandium	21	$1s^22s^22p^63s^23p^63d^14s^2$	Sc^{3+}	$1s^22s^22p^63s^23p^63d^0$
titanium	22	$1s^22s^22p^63s^23p^63d^24s^2$	Ti^{4+}	$1s^22s^22p^63s^23p^63d^0$
zinc	30	$1s^22s^22p^63s^23p^63d^{10}4s^2$	Zn^{2+}	$1s^22s^22p^63s^23p^63d^{10}$
lead	82	$1s^22s^22p^63s^23p^63d^{10}4s^24p^64d^{10}4f^{14}5s^25p^65d^{10}6s^26p^2$	Pb^{2+}	$1s^22s^22p^63s^23p^63d^{10}4s^24p^64d^{10}4f^{14}5s^25p^65d^{10}6s^2$
copper	29	$1s^22s^22p^63s^23p^63d^{10}4s^1$	Cu^+	$1s^22s^22p^63s^23p^63d^{10}$

● **Table 5.3** Electronic configurations

You may be able to try this yourself. Aqueous $[Co(H_2O)_6]^{2+}$ is pink. With care, add to it an excess amount of concentrated hydrochloric acid. The colour changes to blue. The reaction that occurs is:

$$[Co(H_2O)_6]^{2+}(aq) + 4Cl^-(aq) \longrightarrow [CoCl_4]^{2-}(aq) + 6H_2O(l)$$

pink   blue
octahedral   tetrahedral
hexaaquacobalt(II)   tetrachlorocobalt(II)

By changing the ligand, the shape of the complex ion is altered and the energy difference between the d–d orbitals is decreased.

Now add an excess amount of aqueous ammonia to aqueous $[Ni(H_2O)_6]^{2+}$, which is green. The complex ion $[Ni(NH_3)_6]^{2+}$ is formed. This is still octahedral in shape, but is blue in colour. The energy difference between the d–d orbitals is greater than for $[Ni(H_2O)_6]^{2+}$ and a higher frequency of radiation is absorbed, causing the colour change.

The nature of the ligand is the main influence in determining the change in ΔE. It has been found that the order of increasing ΔE in metal-ion complexes is Cl^-, H_2O and NH_3.

SAQ 5.1

A compound shows an absorption band at 490 nm in the visible region of the spectrum. Why does it appear to be red?

SAQ 5.2

When aqueous ammonia is added in excess to an aqueous solution of $[Cu(H_2O)_6]^{2+}$, the following reaction occurs:

$$[Cu(H_2O)_6]^{2+} + 4NH_3 \longrightarrow [Cu(NH_3)_4(H_2O)_2]^{2+} + 4H_2O$$

pale blue   deep blue-violet

Explain why this colour change is observed.

Colour in organic compounds

Why organic compounds are coloured

You will be aware that, whereas many organic compounds are colourless, some have a very distinctive colour. Examples are the yellow aromatic nitro compounds and the strongly coloured large organic molecules that are used as indicators in volumetric analysis.

The colour results from electronic transitions within the molecules, which cause the absorption of a certain frequency of radiation in the visible region of the spectrum, i.e. wavelengths between 400 and 750 nm.

From the section on molecular orbitals (chapter 3), you will know that the interaction of atomic orbitals leads to the formation of bonding and antibonding molecular orbitals. These molecular orbitals are of two types: the sigma (σ) orbital, in which electron density is concentrated along the internuclear axis; and the pi (π) orbital, in which electron density is concentrated on either side of the internuclear axis. The relative energy levels of these orbitals and of the non-bonding orbitals (n) are shown in *figure 3.12*.

In most organic compounds, the bonding and non-bonding orbitals contain electrons and the antibonding orbitals are empty. Electronic transitions between these orbitals result in absorption in the visible region, and reflection of wavelengths in the same region of the spectrum produces colour. All organic compounds absorb radiation to some extent, but most absorb in the ultraviolet region well below 400 nm and so are colourless.

Chromophores

Chromophores are unsaturated groups of atoms in organic compounds that absorb radiation mainly in the ultraviolet and visible regions of the spectrum. Therefore, they give rise to the electronic transitions:

- $\pi \longrightarrow \pi^*$ (pi bonding to pi antibonding)
- $n \longrightarrow \pi^*$ (non-bonding to pi antibonding)

For example, the chromophore $>C=C$ may show an absorption band corresponding to a $\pi \longrightarrow \pi^*$ transition. The $>C=O$ chromophore may show two absorption bands corresponding to the $\pi \longrightarrow \pi^*$ and $n \longrightarrow \pi^*$ transitions.

The absorption frequencies that correspond to these transitions are characteristic of the chromophores and are used for their identification (*table 5.4*).

Chromophore	λ_{max}/nm
$>C=C$	190
$>C=O$	190 and 280
$-C\equiv N$	160
$-N^+\equiv N$	350
$-N^+\underset{O}{\overset{O}{\diagup}}$	270
⬡	190 and 260

● **Table 5.4** Maximum absorption wavelengths of some chromophores

These values are approximate because: they vary with temperature; they are different in various solvents; and they depend on whether there are certain saturated groups, e.g. OH and Cl, nearby. They are also affected by conjugation in molecules (see next section).

Effect of chemical environment on absorption bands of chromophores

The wavelengths and the intensities of the absorption bands due to chromophores are altered by *conjugation* in molecules and *delocalisation* of electrons.

A **conjugated** molecule is one that possesses alternating double and single bonds, for example

1,3-butadiene, $CH_2=CH-CH=CH_2$. A consequence of this bond arrangement is that the electrons do not remain between adjacent carbon atoms, as they do in ethene $CH_2=CH_2$. Instead, they are spread over all the carbon atoms. They are said to become **delocalised**. An example of this occurs in benzene, where the electrons are evenly distributed around the ring (*figure 5.5a*).

Where there is conjugation of chromophores in a molecule, the absorption bands due to the conjugated chromophores are shifted to longer wavelengths and are more intense than those of an isolated chromophore. This occurs because the electrons in the π and π^* orbitals of each chromophore interact with those of another and become delocalised. They form new orbitals, in which the highest-energy π orbital and the lowest-energy π^* orbital are closer together in energy (*figure 5.5b*).

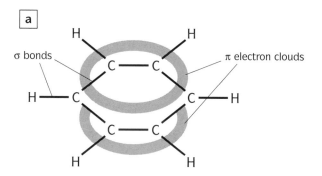

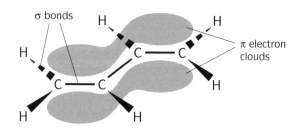

● **Figure 5.5** **a** The structure of benzene, showing delocalisation of π electrons. **b** The conjugation (i.e. joining together) of two ethene chromophores to form 1,3-butadiene. The $\pi \longrightarrow \pi^*$ transition in ethene ($CH_2=CH_2$) occurs at ~175 nm. In the conjugated molecule $CH_2=CH-CH=CH_2$ it occurs at ~210 nm, and the corresponding absorption band is more intense.

Diphenylpolyenes	Number of CH=CH groups (n)	Region of the electronic transition	Colour
$C_6H_5–(CH=CH)_n–C_6H_5$	1 or 2	ultraviolet	colourless
	3	visible	yellow
	15	visible	greenish black

● *Table 5.5*

Effect of additional chromophores

The conjugation of additional chromophores in a molecule will move the wavelength of the absorption band more and more from the ultraviolet towards the visible region of the spectrum (i.e. towards longer wavelengths). The diphenylpolyenes show this 'progression' as the number of (CH=CH) groups in the molecule is increased. This is illustrated in *table 5.5*.

The benzene ring as a chromophore

Benzene may be considered as a special case of a conjugated triene. It shows a relatively weak absorption band due to the $\pi \longrightarrow \pi^*$ transition near 260 nm. When the chromophore NO_2 is substituted in the ring to form nitrobenzene, this band is shifted to a longer wavelength. A new intense absorption band is also observed at a longer wavelength due to the $\pi \longrightarrow \pi^*$ transition in the extended conjugated system. Benzene is colourless, and nitrobenzene is yellow.

Dyes and colour changes in acid–base indicators

Dyes are usually large organic molecules that are coloured because they contain chromophores. For example, when a diazonium salt combines with naphthalene-2-ol, a bright red azo dye is formed:

benzenediazonium chloride   naphthalene-2-ol   red azo dye

The change in colour in some acid–base indicators may be explained in terms of changes in the structure of the molecules. For example, the molecule of methyl orange has a long conjugated system. In alkaline solution this molecule is orange, but in the presence of excess acid the structure is altered and the colour changes to red. This shows that radiation of longer wavelength is now being absorbed (*figure 5.6a*).

Another common indicator, phenolphthalein, is colourless in acid solution, but in the presence of excess alkali the structure changes and the molecule becomes red (*figure 5.6b*).

SAQ 5.3
Name the chromophores in the following compounds and the electronic transitions that may occur between their molecular orbitals:

$C_6H_5COCH_3$ $CH_3CH=CHCHO$
phenylethanone   *trans*-but-2-enal

SAQ 5.4
An organic compound showed absorption bands at $\lambda_{max} = 160$ nm and 190 nm. The composition by mass of the compound is C = 67.9%, H = 5.7% and N = 26.4%. The empirical and molecular formulae are the same. Suggest a possible structure for this compound.

SAQ 5.5
When two similar chromophores are conjugated, the absorption band is shifted to a longer wavelength. Explain what happens to the electrons in the molecular orbitals to cause this effect.

Colorimetric analysis

In colorimetric analysis, we use radiation in the visible region of the spectrum to measure chemical concentrations. Quantitative methods measure the reduction in the intensity of the radiation when it passes through the sample. The measurements are made with a **spectrophotometer**. A simplified form of a spectrophotometer is also used that involves the use of coloured filters. This is called a

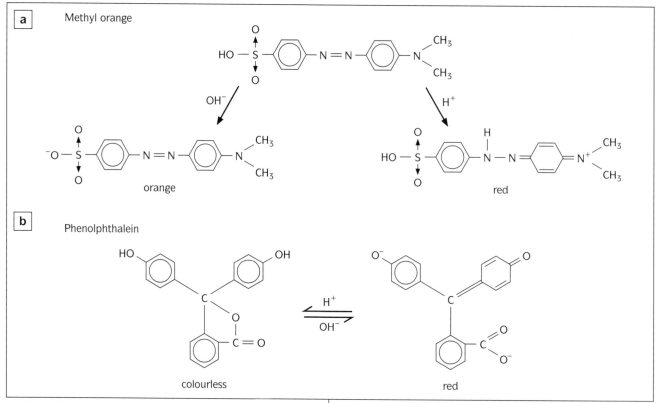

● **Figure 5.6 a** The two chemical structures of methyl orange in the presence of H^+ and OH^-. **b** The two structures of phenolphthalein in the presence of H^+ and OH^-.

colorimeter. *Figure 5.7* shows how these instruments work.

Beer's law

In chapter 4 we used absorbance, $A = \log_{10}(I_0/I)$ to find the concentration of absorbing atoms in a vapour. The method was based on a relationship analogous to Beer's law.

This law relates to samples in solution and is the basis for colorimetric analysis. **Beer's law** states that, when monochromatic radiation (radiation of one wavelength) is passed through a liquid sample, the reduction in the intensity of the radiation depends on the concentration of the absorbing species and on the thickness of the sample. It is obeyed by most substances in dilute solution, i.e. for concentrations less than $0.5\,mol\,dm^{-3}$.

Beer's law is expressed by the equation
$$A = \log_{10}(I_0/I) = \varepsilon cl$$
Where A = **absorbance**, defined as $\log_{10}(I_0/I)$; I_0 = intensity of the incident beam; I = intensity

of the transmitted beam; c = concentration of the solution; l = thickness of the sample, which is also called the **path length**; and ε = a constant called the **molar absorptivity**. The molar absorptivity is the absorbance of a $1\,mol\,dm^{-3}$ solution in a $1\,cm$ cell. The value of ε depends on the wavelength of the incident radiation and on the nature of the absorbing species.

The instruments record absorbance or transmittance. **Transmittance** (symbol T) is the fraction of the incident radiation transmitted. It is defined as I/I_0 and is related to the absorbance A by $A = \log_{10}(1/T)$.

Choice of wavelengths or filters

The wavelength that shows maximum absorption by the sample is used in colorimetric measurements.

■ In spectrophotometers, a diffraction grating or prism (monochromator) isolates this wavelength.

■ In colorimeters, the monochromator is replaced by coloured filters, which allow certain bands of wavelengths to pass into the absorbing species.

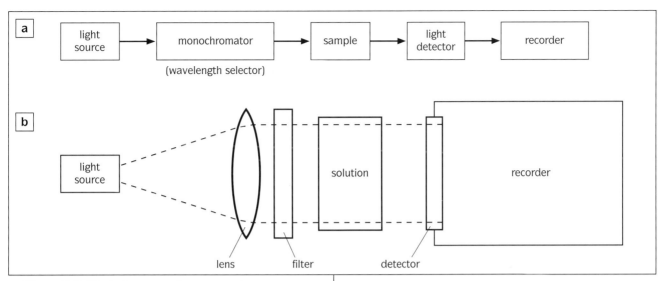

● **Figure 5.7** Block diagrams of **a** spectrophotometer and **b** colorimeter.

A **filter** is made of coloured glass or plastic that has been impregnated with a dye. It transmits radiation only from a specific region of the spectrum and absorbs all the other components. In practice, a filter of the complementary colour to the colour of the solution is chosen. For example, a blue filter is used for red, pink, orange and yellow solutions.

Applications of Beer's law

To find the iron content of blood serum

You saw on page 53 that iron can form a purple complex with ferrozine. The Fe^{3+} ions in blood serum are reduced to the Fe^{2+} state and freed from the protein transferrin. This protein and all other proteins present are precipitated out and removed, leaving the Fe^{2+} ions in solution. When the Fe^{2+} ions are treated with ferrozine, they form $(ferrozine)_3Fe^{II}$. This is a purple complex that shows a maximum absorption band at 562 nm (*figure 5.8*).

When Beer's law holds, a plot of absorbance against concentration gives a straight line passing through the origin with a slope equal to the product $\varepsilon \times l$.

A set of standard solutions each containing a known amount of the $(ferrozine)_3Fe^{II}$ complex are prepared. Their absorbances are measured at

562 nm and a calibration graph is plotted (*figure 5.9*). The absorbance of the serum sample is then measured at the same wavelength. The concentration corresponding to this measured absorbance is read from the calibration graph.

Usually a blank is also measured and subtracted from each absorbance reading. A **blank** may be a solution of all the reagents except the absorbing species, or it may be distilled water.

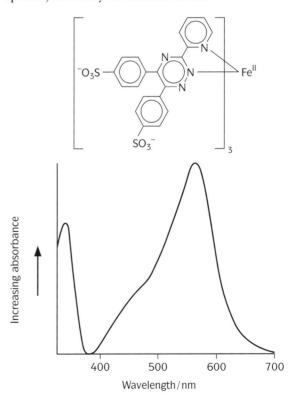

● **Figure 5.8** The absorption spectrum of $(ferrozine)_3Fe^{II}$ and the structure of the complex.

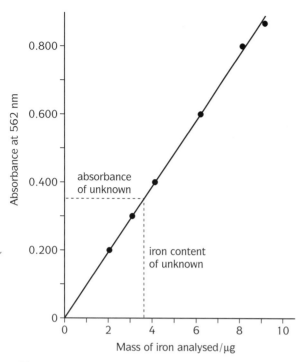

● **Figure 5.9** Calibration graph for determining the iron content of blood serum.

To find the copper content of bronze

Bronze is an alloy of copper and tin. A known quantity of bronze is dissolved in nitric acid. The acid converts the tin into tin(IV) oxide (SnO_2), which is filtered off. The solution is diluted to a known volume with distilled water. The concentration of copper in the solution is determined by absorbance measurements of the pale blue hexaaquacopper(II) ion $[Cu(H_2O)_6]^{2+}$ or the deep blue tetraamminecopper(II) ion $[Cu(NH_3)_4(H_2O)_2]^{2+}$ using standard solutions and a calibration graph.

When Beer's law holds, i.e. when $A = \log_{10}(I_0/I) = \varepsilon cl$:

■ The concentration of a sample may be determined by one absorbance measurement provided the molar absorptivity ε and the path length l are known.
■ The path length l may be calculated from the equation when all the other quantities are known.

To determine the stoichiometry of a complex ion

A pair of chemical species that will form a coloured ion in solution are chosen. For example, Fe^{3+} and CNS^- form a red complex ion:

$$Fe^{3+} + nCNS^- \longrightarrow Fe(CNS)_n^x$$

where x = the charge on the ion and n = the number of ligands.

Equimolar solutions are used. A set of mixtures is prepared by mixing certain volumes of these solutions so that the total volume remains the same and the total number of moles of metal ion and ligand remain the same for each mixture, while their mole ratio changes systematically. Look at *table 5.6*.

The absorbance of each mixture is measured and plotted against the volume fraction of the ligand. Volume fraction is expressed as $V_L/(V_M + V_L)$, where V_M is the volume of the metal-ion solution and V_L is the volume of the ligand solution.

Mixture	*Volume of* $1 \times 10^{-3} mol\,dm^{-3}\,Fe(NO_3)_3,$ V_M/cm^3	*Volume of* $1 \times 10^{-3} mol\,dm^{-3}\,KCNS,$ V_L/cm^3	$\dfrac{V_L}{V_M + V_L}$	*Absorbance at* $\lambda = 455\,nm$
1	9.00	1.00	0.1	0.100
2	8.00	2.00	0.2	0.200
3	7.00	3.00	0.3	0.300
4	6.00	4.00	0.4	0.330
5	5.00	5.00	0.5	0.340
6	4.00	6.00	0.6	0.320
7	3.00	7.00	0.7	0.295
8	2.00	8.00	0.8	0.198
9	1.00	9.00	0.9	0.100

● *Table 5.6*

The resulting curve *(figure 5.10)* shows a maximum, which indicates the metal-to-ligand ratio of the complex in solution. In this case the maximum is at 0.5 on the volume fraction axis, and this shows that the ratio is 1:1, i.e.

$$Fe^{3+} + CNS^- \longrightarrow Fe(CNS)^{2+}$$

If the maximum had occurred at 0.67, the ligand-to-metal ratio would be 2:1; and at 0.75, the ratio would be 3:1.

A colorimetric method of analysis often has advantages over other methods:

- At low concentrations, it gives accurate results.
- In routine analysis, it is simple and quick.
- Sometimes no other method is satisfactory; for example, in the analysis of some biological substances.

SAQ 5.6

What is the main condition for Beer's law to be obeyed?

SAQ 5.7

What filters would you use in a colorimeter to measure the absorption of solutions that are: **a** violet and purple, **b** blue and green?

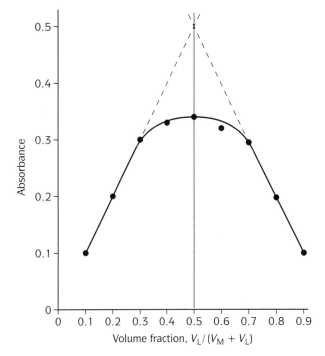

● *Figure 5.10* Graph showing the cation-to-ligand ratio for the complex ion $Fe(CNS)^{2+}$. The experimental plot is a curve. The lines can be extrapolated to meet above the curve at 0.5. The curvature of the experimental lines is due to the complex formation not being complete. The maximum occurs at the volume ratio V_M/V_L corresponding to the combining ratio of cation to ligand.

Questions

1 Describe how colour arises in:
   a transition-element complexes,
   b organic compounds.

2 The following table shows the results obtained when a set of standard solutions of a coloured substance were measured with a colorimeter:

I	88.7	79.5	70.7	63.3	56.4	50.2
I_0	100	100	100	100	100	100
Percentage concentration	0.01	0.02	0.03	0.04	0.05	0.06

Plot a calibration graph using these data. Find the concentration of a solution of the same substance for which the value of I is 76.0.

3 Cu^{2+} ions form a coloured complex with a ligand L. Using the absorbance data in the table below, find the cation-to-ligand ratio in this complex.

Mixture	Volume of 8.00×10^{-5} mol dm^{-3} $CuSO_4/cm^3$	Volume of 8.00×10^{-5} mol dm^{-3} ligand L/cm^3	Absorbance
1	9.00	1.00	0.104
2	8.00	2.00	0.210
3	7.00	3.00	0.314
4	6.00	4.00	0.419
5	5.00	5.00	0.507
6	4.00	6.00	0.571
7	3.00	7.00	0.574
8	2.00	8.00	0.423
9	1.00	9.00	0.211

SUMMARY

- Ultraviolet and visible spectroscopy is based on energy changes that occur within molecules and ions when radiation from the ultraviolet and visible regions of the spectrum is absorbed. Transition-element complexes and organic compounds are studied by ultraviolet and visible spectroscopy, which is particularly useful for quantitative analysis.

- Transition-element ions are strongly polarising and attract molecules and ions that have lone-pairs of electrons (ligands) and form coordinate bonds with them. The lone-pair electrons are accepted into the empty 3d, 4s and 4p orbitals of the metal ions. Thus, complex metal ions are formed.

- The complex metal ion has five degenerate d orbitals (i.e. orbitals of equal energy). When the ligands approach the ion, the d orbitals split into two energy groups. An electron can now be promoted from the lower to the higher energy level. This is known as a d–d transition. The energy required for the transition, ΔE, is so small that absorption of radiation in the visible region of the spectrum will make it occur. The remaining components of the visible radiation are reflected and give the complex its colour. One requirement for this transition is that the d orbitals must have at least one unpaired electron.

- The magnitude of ΔE determines the colour of the complex ion. If one ligand is replaced by another, ΔE is altered and so is the colour. For example, $[Ni(H_2O)_6]^{2+}$ is green and $[Ni(NH_3)_6]^{2+}$ is blue.

- In most organic compounds, the bonding and non-bonding orbitals contain electrons and the antibonding orbitals are empty. Absorption of radiation in the visible region of the spectrum causes electronic transitions between these orbitals. Reflection of the remaining wavelengths, in the same region of the spectrum, gives the compounds their colours. Many organic compounds absorb ultraviolet radiation and so are colourless.

- Chromophores are unsaturated groups in organic compounds that absorb radiation mainly in the ultraviolet and visible regions of the spectrum and give rise to electronic transitions; an example of a chromophore is $>C=O$. The frequencies of the transitions are characteristic of the chemical groups and are used for their identification.

- The wavelengths and the intensities of the absorption bands due to chromophores are altered by conjugation in molecules and by the delocalisation of electrons. This is seen in acid–base indicators, when the colour changes on going from alkaline to acid conditions. This colour change occurs because the structures of the molecules alter and radiation of a different wavelength is being absorbed.

- Colorimetric analysis is based on the absorption of visible radiation. Beer's law is used to find the concentration of dilute coloured solutions. A set of standard solutions is used. Their absorbances and that of the unknown solution are measured. A calibration graph is drawn and the concentration of the unknown solution is read from the graph.

- The stoichiometry of coloured complex ions is also determined by absorption measurements in the visible region of the spectrum.

Chapter six

Infrared spectroscopy

By the end of this chapter you should be able to:

1 explain the origin of infrared absorption of simple molecules, including the need for a dipole moment, and using H_2O, CO, CO_2 and SO_2 as examples;

2 identify characteristic absorptions in the infrared spectrum of a compound containing up to two functional groups from $C-O$, $C=C$, $C=O$, OH, NH_2, CN and $C-Cl$;

3 suggest structures for a compound from its infrared spectrum (simple molecules with up to three functional groups);

4 describe how samples of liquids and solids can be prepared for infrared analysis (liquid films, solutions, mulls and halide discs) and outline the advantages and disadvantages of each;

5 show awareness of the use of infrared spectroscopy in analysis in, for example, quality control, monitoring breath alcohol, paint analysis and monitoring air pollution.

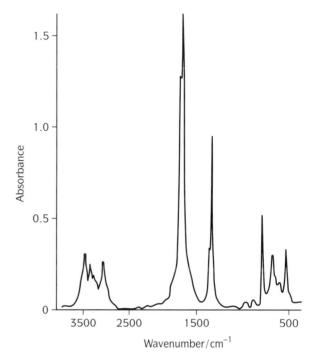

● **Figure 6.1** The infrared spectrum of calcium oxalate monohydrate.

Introduction

We can identify most organic and inorganic compounds by infrared (i.r.) spectroscopy. With a few exceptions, each type of molecule has a unique infrared spectrum. By matching the spectrum of an unknown molecule with the spectra of known compounds, the unknown molecule can be identified. For example, kidney (renal) stones may consist of pure calcium phosphate, or they may contain a mixture of calcium oxalate and calcium phosphate, or they may be complex mixtures of up to six components. Analysis of these stones by infrared spectroscopy is used to find the cause of their formation, which may be due simply to low liquid intake or more seriously to kidney failure.

Infrared spectroscopy is less useful for quantitative analysis than is ultraviolet and visible spectroscopy. This is because the narrow peaks of the infrared spectrum (*figure 6.1*) lead to small

differences from Beer's law, and also the measurements are less precise. Fortunately, there are many applications where a high level of precision is not required, and the technique has been adapted to follow the progress of some industrial processes. *Figure 6.2* shows part of the infrared spectrum of beer during fermentation. The three spectra show the changes that occur in beer wort as the brewers' yeast in the wort mixture turns the sugars into alcohol.

Absorption of infrared radiation by simple molecules

You have seen in chapter 3 that the atoms in a molecule vibrate and absorb infrared radiation in a quantised manner to form the infrared spectrum.

Not *all* vibrations between atoms cause absorption. Those which do cause absorption are known

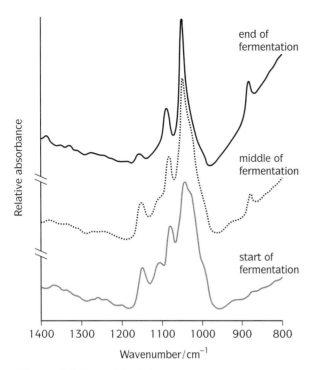

● **Figure 6.2** Part of the infrared spectrum of beer at three stages during fermentation.

as **infrared-active modes** of vibration. For a vibration to be infrared-active, it must change the dipole moment of the bond.

Dipole moment

In *Foundation Chemistry* you saw how a dipole forms in an atom or molecule when there is an imbalance in the distribution of electrons around that atom or molecule. The extent of the unequal sharing of bonding electrons in a molecule is represented by its **dipole moment**. HCl has a dipole moment because chlorine is more **electronegative** than hydrogen (see *Foundation Chemistry*, chapter 3) and the molecule may be represented as $H^{\delta+}-Cl^{\delta-}$. The dipole moment is defined as the product of the size of the charges and the distance separating them *(figure 6.3)*.

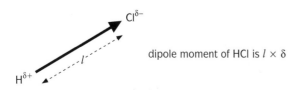

● **Figure 6.3** The dipole moment of HCl as a vector.

How the infrared radiation is absorbed

The process is as follows:

■ When a bond vibrates normally, as in HCl, it is stretched along the line joining the nuclei of the two atoms.

■ The vibration causes the electron distribution around the atoms to change, so the dipole moment also changes (it is said to **fluctuate**).

■ A molecule with a fluctuating dipole moment can interact with electromagnetic radiation and absorb energy from it.

■ This increases the energy of vibration and raises the molecule to a higher vibrational energy level.

A molecule can absorb radiation only if there is a net change in the dipole moment during a particular vibration. Most polyatomic molecules (i.e. molecules with more than two atoms) fulfil this condition. A few molecules such as H_2, O_2, N_2 and Cl_2, which do not have a dipole moment, cannot absorb infrared radiation.

Modes of vibration

The number of ways in which a molecule may vibrate are known as its **modes of vibration**. Look at *figure 6.4*, which shows how atoms in different molecules move for each vibration.

In carbon monoxide, there is only *one* mode of vibration, the stretching of the bond, and so *one* absorption band is seen. Water and sulphur dioxide are bent molecules. Bonds stretch and angles change as the molecules vibrate and distort. They have *three* modes of vibration and show *three* absorption bands *(figure 6.5a)*. Carbon dioxide has *four* modes of vibration but shows only *two* absorption bands. This is because the symmetrical stretching of the linear molecule does not cause a change in the dipole moment, and so no absorption occurs for this mode of vibration. Also, the two bending modes of vibration absorb at the *same* frequency. They are said to be **degenerate** and form only one absorption band *(figure 6.5b)*.

Infrared spectroscopy is used for finding the shape or symmetry of molecules. For example, if a

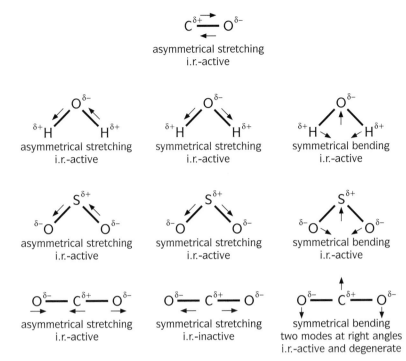

● **Figure 6.4** The modes of vibration for carbon monoxide (CO), water (H₂O), sulphur dioxide (SO₂) and carbon dioxide (CO₂). The modes are labelled as symmetrical or asymmetrical, and as infrared-active or infrared-inactive.

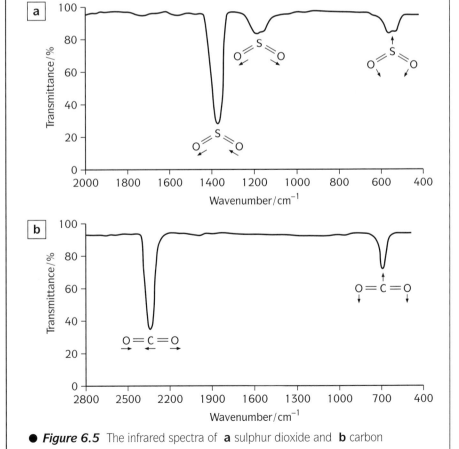

● **Figure 6.5** The infrared spectra of **a** sulphur dioxide and **b** carbon dioxide.

linear or bent (non-linear) structure is assumed for a molecule, the number of infrared-active vibrations can be found for each proposed shape and would equal the number of absorption bands expected. Examination of the infrared spectrum would show which is the correct structure for the molecule.

SAQ 6.1

Explain why carbon monoxide has a dipole moment.

SAQ 6.2

a Draw the possible modes of vibration for the nitrogen dioxide molecule, assuming both a linear and an angular structure.

b The infrared spectrum of nitrogen dioxide shows three absorption bands. What does this tell you about the symmetry of the molecule?

The infrared spectrum

Figure 6.6a shows how the infrared spectrophotometer works. The spectrum of butanal (*figure 6.6b*) shows absorption bands represented in wavenumbers. In infrared analysis, wavenumbers are used for convenience instead of frequency or wavelength.

A **wavenumber** is the reciprocal of wavelength, and the convention is to quote wavenumbers in cm^{-1}. The symbol for wavenumber is $\tilde{v}$:

$$\tilde{v} = 1/\lambda$$

In chapter 3 you saw that frequency $f = c/\lambda$. To find the frequency (in s^{-1}) from the

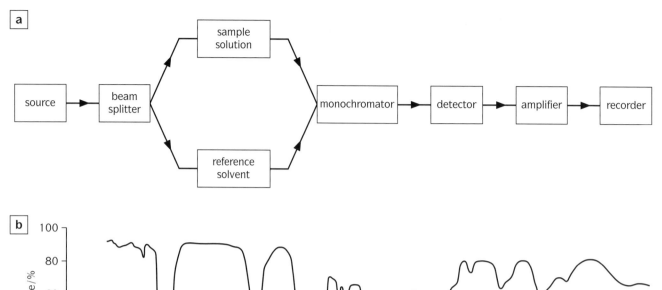

● *Figure 6.6* **a** A double-beam infrared spectrophotometer. This is used to analyse solids in solution. The monochromator selects radiation of a particular frequency. The detector compares the intensities of the sample and reference beams. The differences between these intensities is amplified and then recorded on a chart. **b** The infrared spectrum of butanal, $CH_3CH_2CH_2CHO$.

wavenumber, multiply the wavenumber $\tilde{v}$ by c (in $cm\,s^{-1}$):

$$f = c/\lambda \quad \text{so} \quad f = c\tilde{v} \quad \text{where } \tilde{v} = 1/\lambda$$

For example, a wavenumber of $17\,000$ cm^{-1} corresponds to a frequency given by

$$f = \tilde{v} \times c$$
$$= 17\,000\,cm^{-1} \times 3.00 \times 10^{10}\,cm\,s^{-1}$$
$$= 5.1 \times 10^{14}\,s^{-1}$$

Applications of infrared spectroscopy

Qualitative analysis

We use infrared spectroscopy to identify unknown compounds. It is particularly useful in organic chemistry, because very similar compounds, such as isomers, have different spectra and can be distinguished from one another. Also, functional groups (e.g. OH in alcohol) and other bonds such as C–H can be identified. Each infrared-active vibration in a molecule causes an absorption band to be formed in the spectrum at a characteristic wavenumber. These characteristic values are listed in *table 6.1*.

When identifying an unknown compound, it is useful to look first for the presence of functional groups. These will help to **classify** it, i.e. determine what *type* of compound it is. The region between 1500 and 3500 cm^{-1} shows the characteristic bands arising from the functional groups and some other bonds. Compare the wavenumbers of the absorption bands in this region of the spectrum of butanal *(figure 6.6b)* with the characteristic values for absorptions in *table 6.1*.

When the compound has been classified, e.g. as an aldehyde or a ketone, we then compare the

Bond	Wavenumber/cm⁻¹
C–Cl	700–800
C–O alcohols, ethers, esters	1000–1300
C=C	1610–1680
C=O aldehydes, ketones, acids, esters	1680–1750
C≡C	2070–2250
C≡N	2200–2280
O–H 'hydrogen-bonded' in acids	2500–3300
C–H alkanes, alkenes, arenes	2840–3095
O–H 'hydrogen-bonded' in alcohols, phenols	3230–3550
N–H primary amines	3350–3500
O–H 'free'	3580–3670

● **Table 6.1** Characteristic ranges for infrared absorption due to stretching vibrations in organic molecules

Compound	Characteristic wavenumber/cm⁻¹
aliphatic ketones	1710–1720
aromatic ketones	1680–1700
carboxylic acids (monomer)	1750–1770
carboxylic acids (dimer)	1710–1720
aliphatic amides	1630–1700
acid chlorides	1790–1815

● **Table 6.2** Effect of chemical environment on the infrared absorption of C=O

whole spectrum with that of known compounds of that class. The most useful part of the spectrum at this stage is between 700 and 1500 cm⁻¹. This is known as the **fingerprint region**, because compounds give a unique set of absorption bands in this area.

Infrared absorption wavenumbers also vary with the chemical environment of the vibrating bond. This is shown for the C=O functional group in *table 6.2*.

Suggesting structures from infrared spectra

Figure 6.7 shows how the spectrum of an organic compound indicates its chemical structure. Look at *table 6.1*. The absorption band between 1610 and 1680 cm⁻¹ indicates the presence of a C=C group. The band between 2200 and 2280 cm⁻¹ shows that the compound contains a C≡N group. The band between 2840 and 3095 cm⁻¹ shows the presence of a C–H bond. From this evidence, we may suggest that the compound is an unsaturated nitrile.

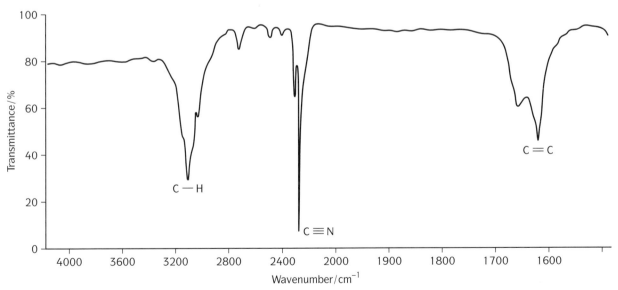

● **Figure 6.7** The infrared spectrum of an organic compound. By studying the positions of the absorption bands, we could suggest that it is propenenitrile CH_2CHCN; its formula can also be written as

SAQ 6.3

Figure 6.8 is the infrared spectrum of an organic compound. Using *table 6.1*, identify the bonds responsible for the absorptions on the spectrum and classify the compound.

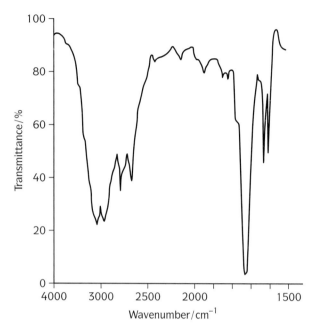

● **Figure 6.8** The infrared spectrum of an unknown organic compound – but which one?

Quantitative analysis

Infrared radiation is used for quantitative analysis by determining the concentration of one of the functional groups in a compound. For example, with a mixture of an alcohol and an alkane, the extent of the absorption of the O–H bond in the alcohol is measured. The method is used in the food industry for quality control. For example, the fat, lactose and protein contents of skimmed milk and whole milk are determined by infrared spectroscopy.

Preparing samples for infrared analysis

A number of different procedures have been developed so that all kinds of substances may be analysed. Glass containers may *not* be used since glass is not transparent to infrared radiation. **Alkali halides**, such as sodium chloride or potassium bromide, which do not absorb infrared radiation, are used instead.

Liquid samples

Pure liquids are examined 'neat' (i.e. undiluted) by placing a thin film of the liquid between two plates of alkali halide or placing the liquid in a cell made of alkali halide, and passing infrared radiation through it. A drawing and photographs of typical liquid cells are shown in *figures 6.9a* and *b*.

Solutions are made using solvents that are transparent to infrared radiation, such as tetra-chloromethane and trichloromethane. As for pure liquids, the solution is placed in a cell made from one of the suitable halides. One disadvantage of this method is that the organic liquids must be completely free of water, which would dissolve the material of the cell and cause the surface to become opaque. This could lead to inaccurate results.

Gaseous samples

Samples of gases are analysed by placing the gas in a relatively large cell with both ends made from the alkali halide. Some gas cells are shown in *figure 6.9c*.

Solid samples

The solid is ground to a powder and mixed with a viscous hydrocarbon (named Nujol) to give a dispersion called a **mull**. The mull is made into a thin film by compressing it between alkali halide plates and the radiation is passed through them, using a cell like that in *figure 6.9d*. This method has the disadvantage that Nujol absorbs infrared radiation and forms its own spectrum. The spectrum of pure Nujol must also be recorded, so that its absorption bands may be recognised on the spectrum of the powdered sample. The difference between the two spectra is the spectrum of the pure compound. An example is shown in *figures 6.9e–g*.

There is another method that has the advantage of giving the pure spectrum of a solid sample. First, the finely powdered sample is mixed with dry powdered potassium bromide. Then the mixture is compressed into a very thin disc with a powerful press. Infrared radiation is passed through the disc. Since the potassium bromide is non-absorbing, the spectrum of the sample only will be recorded.

● **Figure 6.9** **a** A simplified 'exploded' view of a typical cell used for liquids. The plates (cell windows) are about 40 mm × 25 mm, and the thickness of the liquid sample is between 0.015 mm and 1.0 mm. **b** Some liquid cells. **c** Some gas cells. **d** Two mull cells. **e** The infrared spectrum of potassium benzoate in a Nujol mull. **f** The infrared spectrum of Nujol alone. **g** The infrared spectrum of potassium benzoate can be obtained by subtraction of the Nujol spectrum (**f**) from the combined spectrum (**e**).

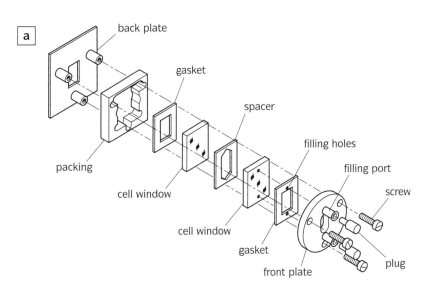

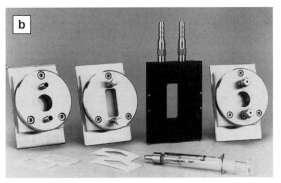

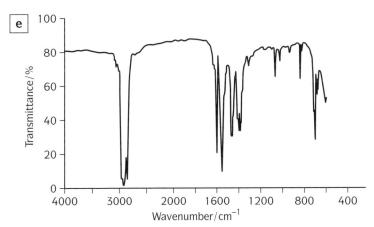

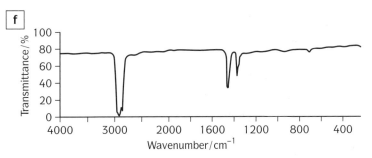

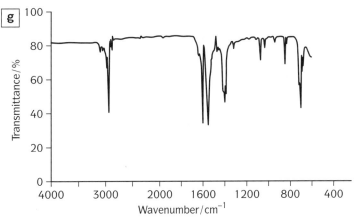

Infrared analysis

In this chapter you have already seen some examples of the use of infrared spectroscopy. However, the applications are numerous and varied, and are being continually extended. Some are listed below.

■ In manufacturing industry, raw materials are checked for purity, the composition of a product is determined and the products of competitors are analysed. For example, it is possible to show if an expensive beeswax has been diluted with a cheaper petroleum wax.

■ In the paint industry, paints and solvents are identified. For example, a scraping of paint from a crashed motor car will provide information on the make and age of the car.

■ Gas streams in industrial processes are monitored. Pollutants in the atmosphere, such as carbon monoxide, sulphur dioxide and nitrobenzene, are identified. Their concentrations are determined to ensure that they satisfy the regulations for safe, clean air.

■ The breath alcohol levels of drivers suspected of having had too much to drink are analysed by the police. The quantity of alcohol in a person's breath depends on the concentration of alcohol in their blood. The breath sample is exposed to infrared radiation in an intoximeter – the 'breathalyser' *(figure 6.10a)*. Alcohol has a distinctive infrared spectrum *(figure 6.10b)*. The peak at 2950 cm^{-1} is isolated by filters for quantitative analysis. The size of the peak depends on how much radiation has been absorbed by the alcohol. This in turn depends on the amount of alcohol in the breath sample.

■ Lastly, but most important to the progress of science, infrared analysis is used by research chemists to classify and identify the products of their work.

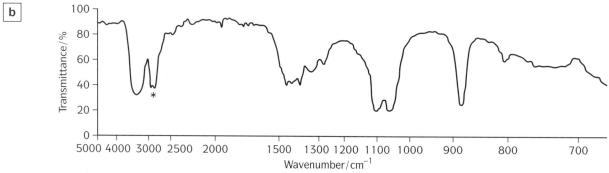

● **Figure 6.10 a** Alcohol levels in your breath may be measured with an intoximeter – the 'breathalyser'. **b** The infrared spectrum of ethanol CH$_3$CH$_2$OH. The 'peak' at 2950 cm^{-1} (marked by a star) is the one analysed in the intoximeter.

SUMMARY

- Infrared spectroscopy is based on the fact that, when a bond between atoms in a molecule vibrates, it changes the dipole moment. Infrared radiation may be absorbed as a result and an absorption spectrum may be recorded.

- Polyatomic molecules vibrate in a number of ways. Only the modes of vibration that are associated with a changing dipole moment will give absorption bands.

- The shape and symmetry of a triatomic molecule may be determined. Find the number of vibrations that could give absorption bands for each proposed structure and compare the possible bands with the infrared spectrum of the molecule.

- Infrared spectra are used for identifying unknown organic and inorganic compounds by comparing their spectra with those of known compounds. The fingerprint region of the spectrum, in which compounds give a unique set of absorption bands, is most useful for this purpose.

- Functional groups in organic molecules are identified by the position of their absorption bands on the infrared spectrum. The characteristic absorption frequencies for functional groups in different chemical environments are known, and complete spectra have been recorded for many compounds. They are widely used for classification and identification.

- Infrared spectroscopy is used in the chemical analysis of a great variety of solids, liquids and gases. It also has some quantitative applications, e.g. in quality control and monitoring gases.

Questions

1 Explain why samples analysed by infrared radiation should be free of water.

2 Compare and contrast infrared spectroscopy with ultraviolet and visible spectroscopy under the four headings: **a** Principles, **b** Instrumentation, **c** Applications, and **d** Advantages and disadvantages.

Chapter seven

Nuclear magnetic resonance spectroscopy

By the end of this chapter you should be able to:

1 outline in simple terms the principles of proton (^{1}H) nuclear magnetic resonance;

2 describe the basic features of a nuclear magnetic resonance spectrometer;

3 explain how the chemical environment of a proton affects the magnetic field that it experiences, and hence the absorption of energy at resonance, and explain the use of the δ scale and TMS as a standard;

4 describe the effects of adjacent protons on the magnetic field experienced by a given proton;

5 predict, from a nuclear magnetic resonance spectrum, the number of protons in each group present in a given molecule (integration of peak area giving the relative numbers of ^{1}H present);

6 predict, from a nuclear magnetic resonance spectrum, the number of protons adjacent to a given proton, using spin–spin splitting as a diagnostic tool;

7 suggest, from a nuclear magnetic resonance spectrum, possible structures for a molecule containing up to three functional groups;

8 describe how the addition of D_2O may be used to identify labile protons;

9 outline the use of nuclear magnetic resonance spectroscopy as an important diagnostic tool in medicine in body scanners.

Introduction

When a new chemical reaction is carried out in a research laboratory and an organic product is formed, the first questions asked are: What is it? What is its structure? These questions are answered by recording and interpreting nuclear magnetic resonance (n.m.r.) spectra.

A proton (^{1}H) n.m.r. spectrum will tell us which hydrogen-containing groups are present in a molecule. For example, the hydrogen atoms in benzene rings or in methyl groups can be identified and multiple bonds can be detected.

The analytical value of n.m.r. spectroscopy was shown by proving the innocence of a chemist who attempted to make an air-freshener spray and produced instead, by mistake, 1.3 kg of the illicit drug 'Ecstasy' worth £400 000 (*figure 7.1*).

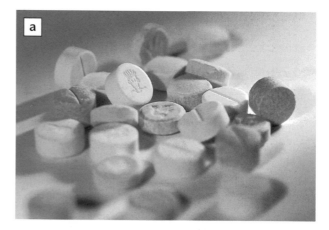

● *Figure 7.1* 'Ecstasy' is an illicit drug, considered dangerous by many people. Its manufacture starts from isosafrole. The fragrances in some air-freshener sprays and cosmetics are based on safrole or isosafrole. Small differences in structure or in reaction conditions can lead to very different products. So it is important to know exactly what you have got at the end of your process. This is where n.m.r. spectroscopy helps.

The starting material chosen for the production of the air spray was an oil called *safrole,* and the starting material for the production of 'Ecstasy' is its isomer *isosafrole.* The chemist had previously attempted an isomerisation reaction to change safrole into isosafrole, which has other uses, for example in the fragrance industry. His laboratory test on the product of the isomerisation indicated that the method had not worked. So he used what he believed to be safrole to produce the air spray. Police who raided his laboratory found that 'Ecstasy' had been produced instead.

During the enquiry that followed, the isomerisation was repeated on the chemist's starting material. Using n.m.r. spectroscopy, it was shown that his isomerisation method had been largely successful, yielding 70% isosafrole, and that the end-product of his process was 'Ecstasy'. After 18 months on remand in prison, the chemist was released on the grounds that sufficiently sophisticated equipment was not available to him to analyse his starting material and final product; his mistake was genuine. After his release he said that he was 'euphoric to be free at last'.

N.m.r. spectroscopy resembles the spectroscopic methods you met in previous chapters because it also depends on the absorption and emission of energy associated with transitions between energy levels.

But n.m.r. differs from these other methods in one important respect. In chapter 3 you saw that, in atomic and molecular spectroscopy, it is the *electrons* that undergo the transitions. In n.m.r. spectroscopy, it is the *atomic nuclei* that undergo the transitions.

In the atomic nucleus, protons and neutrons have almost the same mass, but the proton carries a positive charge whereas the neutron is neutral. Nuclei consisting of an odd number of protons, or an odd number of neutrons, or both, are charged and possess spin. Examples of such nuclei are ^1H, ^{13}C and ^{14}N. These nuclei behave like tiny magnets, which can interact with electromagnetic radiation and produce n.m.r. spectra.

Magnetic fields

A **magnetic field** is represented by lines of force. These lines show the *direction* of the force that a magnetic *north* pole would feel at any point in that magnetic field. The lines of force go from the north pole to the south pole. A magnetic field is described in terms of a **magnetic flux**. The word 'flux' indicates *flow*. We think of magnetic flux flowing from the north pole of the magnet to the south pole. The lines of force are the flux lines, and the strength of the magnetic field is described as the **magnetic flux density**. The field is strongest where the lines are close together – high flux density. The field is weakest where the lines are far apart – low flux density.

The symbol B is used for magnetic flux density, and the unit of magnetic flux density is the tesla (symbol T).

As we will see, there are magnetic fields surrounding spinning protons. These magnetic fields can interact with an external applied magnetic field, and cause effects that we can observe.

The magnetic properties of the proton, ^1H

We will examine the proton, ^1H, here because it is the simplest nucleus and is widely used in n.m.r. analysis. But before we do, we will need to be familiar with some physics – the basic ideas behind magnetic fields. These can be found in the *box.*

When the positively charged proton spins about its own axis, it generates a circulating electric current. In turn, this current produces a magnetic field. The rotating proton is now behaving like a small bar magnet (*figure 7.2a*).

In the absence of an *external* magnetic field, the protons can spin in opposite directions and have the same energy. But when the protons are placed in an external magnetic field, they become aligned in two different orientations: they are aligned with or opposed to the field (*figure 7.2b*).

These two orientations have slightly different energy levels. The protons are **quantised**. The aligned position is at a lower energy level than the opposed position (*figure 7.2c*). If the protons are now irradiated with a suitable frequency of electromagnetic radiation, they interact with it.

■ Some of the lower-energy protons absorb radiation and move to a higher energy level. In doing so, they change their orientation from being *aligned* with the field to being *opposed* to it.

■ At the same time, some of the protons in the higher energy level emit energy and move to the lower level. They also change their orientation: from being *opposed* to the field to being *aligned* with it.

The energy difference between the two nuclear levels (or states) is very small *(figure 7.2c)*. The two energy levels are almost equally populated at room temperature, with the lower energy level containing slightly more nuclei than the upper level. Consequently, overall there is a net absorption of energy because of the small excess of nuclei at the lower level.

The upwards and downwards transitions between the energy levels is the **resonance condition**. Resonance is detected by observing the absorption of the radiation.

Radiofrequency radiation

Radio waves are used in n.m.r. spectroscopy. Radio waves have a frequency of 10–100 MHz ($1\,MHz = 10^6\,Hz = 10^6\,s^{-1}$), which corresponds to a wavelength of 30–3 m. They are the lowest-energy radiation used in analytical chemistry. Their energy is too small to vibrate, rotate or excite an atom

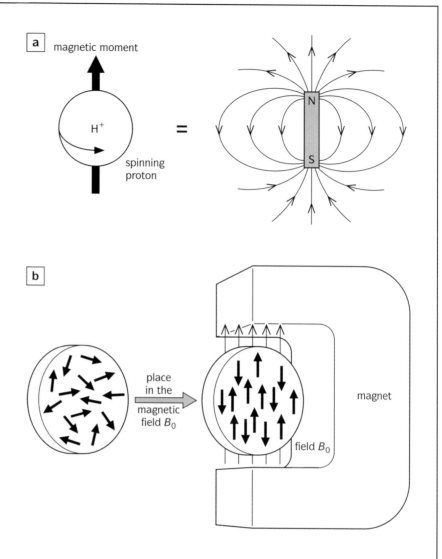

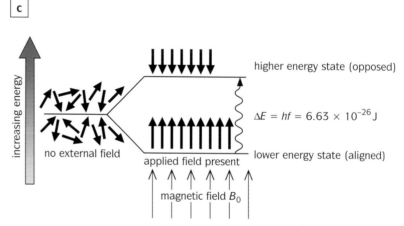

● **Figure 7.2** **a** A spinning proton has a magnetic moment, and will behave like a small bar magnet. **b** Protons are randomly oriented in the absence of an applied external magnetic field. When placed in an applied external magnetic field, they become aligned with or opposed to that field. **c** The aligned and opposed orientations correspond to slightly different energy levels. The energy gap ΔE is given by $\Delta E = hf = 6.63 \times 10^{-26}$ J in an external magnetic field of 2.35 T.

or molecule, but it is large enough to 'flip over' the small nuclear magnet in an applied magnetic field from one orientation to the other.

The radio frequency at which resonance occurs is different for each element and isotope. But the energy levels themselves vary directly with the strength of the applied magnetic field. Consequently, an external magnetic field is chosen to give absorption peaks in a suitable radio-frequency range. Look at *table 7.1* and *table 7.2*.

Nucleus	f/MHz	ΔE/J
^{1}H	100	6.6×10^{-26}
^{13}C	25	1.7×10^{-26}
^{14}N	7	0.5×10^{-26}

● **Table 7.1** Resonance frequencies and corresponding ΔE values for nuclei in an external magnetic field of 2.35 T

Magnetic field, B_0/T	f/MHz	ΔE/J
4.70	200	13.26×10^{-26}
2.35	100	6.63×10^{-26}
1.40	60	3.98×10^{-26}

● **Table 7.2** Relationships between magnetic field strength, resonance frequency and ΔE for ^{1}H

Nuclear magnetic resonance spectrometer

Figure 7.3a shows how an n.m.r. spectrometer works.

■ A liquid sample is held in a glass tube, which is transparent to the radiation.
■ Solid samples are dissolved in a solvent such as trichloromethane or tetrachloromethane, or they may be analysed in the solid state.

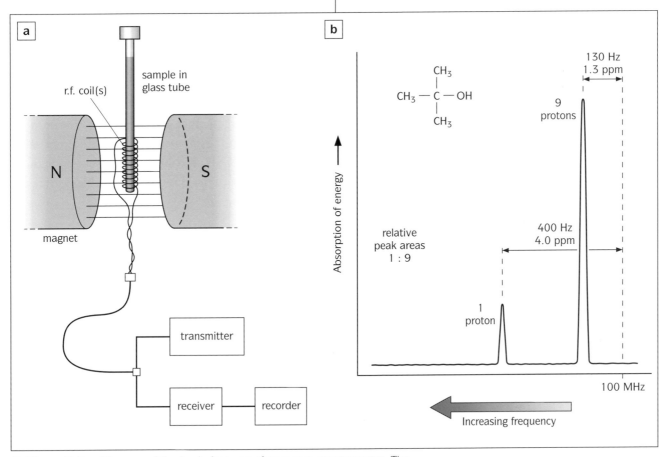

● **Figure 7.3 a** Diagram of the basic features of an n.m.r. spectrometer. The magnetic field between the poles of the magnet is 2.35 T. **b** The n.m.r. spectrum of 2-methylpropan-2-ol. The position of the 100 MHz reference frequency is shown. The peaks are due to the nine equivalent protons in the three –CH$_3$ groups and to the single proton in the –OH group.

- The sample is spun rapidly to ensure that all the magnetic nuclei experience the same magnetic field.
- For a proton n.m.r. spectrum (*figure 7.3b*), the external magnetic field is kept constant with $B_0 = 2.35\,T$. The radio frequency is tuned to 100 MHz and varied in that region.
- When the radio frequency exactly matches the proton energy level gap ΔE, the protons come into resonance and an absorption peak is recorded.
- The spectrum is a plot of radiofrequency energy absorbed against radio frequency.
- Spectra can be obtained with very small samples. As little as $0.5\,cm^3$ of a liquid is required, and the concentration of a solution need not exceed $10^{-3}\,mol\,dm^{-3}$.

Chemical shift

So far, we have examined the resonance of a single proton in isolation from other particles. But in compounds, protons exist in different chemical environments, which cause small changes in their resonance frequencies. Look again at *figure 7.3b*. In 2-methylpropan-2-ol, the nine protons in the methyl groups are in the same chemical environment, and their resonance frequency is 130 Hz higher than the reference frequency of 100 MHz. The proton in the hydroxy group is in a different chemical environment, and its resonance frequency is 400 Hz higher than 100 MHz. The differences between these frequencies and the reference frequency of 100 MHz, i.e. the values 130 and 400 Hz, are called **chemical shifts** and are given the symbol δ. The δ value for the protons in the methyl groups is quoted with reference to 100 MHz as follows: 1.3 ppm, i.e. 1.3 parts per million in 100 million hertz (it is 130 Hz in 100 MHz, or 130 hertz in 100 million hertz, or 1.3 hertz per million hertz in 100 million hertz). Similarly δ for the proton in the OH group is quoted as 4 ppm.

Note that protons in the same group, e.g. CH_3, are **equivalent**. They act together as a group. Also the *area* under each absorption peak is proportional to the *number* of protons in a given environment.

For example, for 2-methylpropan-2-ol, the ratio of the areas of the two proton peaks is 1:9.

How chemical shift occurs

Protons in different environments are surrounded by different patterns of orbiting electrons. When a compound is placed in an external magnetic field, these electrons can **shield** the protons slightly from it. This occurs because a small magnetic field is set up in opposition to the applied field B_0. The protons are then exposed to a *smaller* resultant magnetic field.

You saw earlier (page 75) that the resonance energy gap ΔE varies directly with the magnitude of the applied magnetic field. So does the frequency at which the protons come into resonance:

$$\Delta E = hf \quad \text{and} \quad f \propto B_0$$

The smaller the applied magnetic field, the lower the frequency required for resonance.

In 2-methylpropan-2-ol, the protons on the $-CH_3$ groups are shielded more than the proton on the $-OH$ group because oxygen is more electronegative than carbon and attracts electrons away from the proton. The two types of proton then come into resonance at slightly different radio frequencies. Thus **shielding** leads to lower chemical shift values, and the opposite **de-shielding** leads to higher values.

The standard, TMS

In practice, we measure chemical shifts by reference to the proton resonance of tetramethylsilane (TMS) (*figure 7.4a*). This compound has 12 highly shielded protons in identical environments, and it produces a single resonance peak well separated from most other proton resonances. It is also chemically inert and soluble in most organic compounds.

The method is as follows. The sample is mixed with a small amount of TMS and the spectrum of the mixture is recorded (*figure 7.4b*). The chemical shift of a proton in a molecule of the sample is then defined as

$$\delta = \frac{f - f_0}{f_0} \times 10^6\,ppm$$

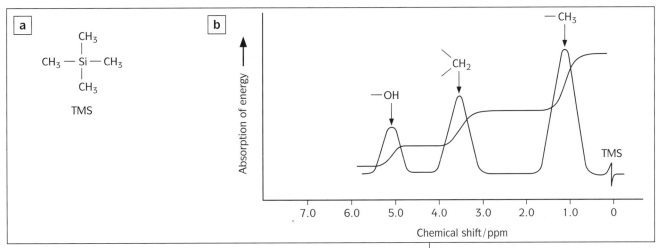

● **Figure 7.4** **a** The structure of tetramethylsilane (TMS). **b** The low-resolution n.m.r. spectrum of ethanol CH_3CH_2OH, showing three peaks. The step-like trace (which is recorded by the peak area integrator) represents the areas under the absorption peaks and shows the ratio of the different types of protons in the molecule. Here they are in the ratio of 3:2:1.

Here f is the frequency at which the protons in the sample come into resonance, and f_0 is the frequency at which the protons in TMS come into resonance.

N.m.r. instruments are designed so that the operating frequency will bring TMS into resonance. When δ is positive, the shift is to a higher frequency. On the δ scale, the chemical shift of TMS is defined as zero. The δ values of most protons in organic molecules fall within the range of 0 to 15 ppm (table 7.3).

The n.m.r. spectrometer also has a peak area integrator. The step heights of the peaks are traced to show the ratios of the different types of proton (figure 7.4b).

Low- and high-resolution n.m.r. spectra

Low-resolution n.m.r. spectrum of ethanol

Look at figure 7.4b again. We can now identify some important features in the spectrum of ethanol, CH_3–CH_2–OH.

■ The three peaks show that there are three different types of proton in three different environments in the molecule.

■ We can compare the chemical shift values in table 7.3 with those on the spectrum to confirm the identity of –CH_3, –CH_2 and –OH.

■ The integrated areas under the peaks are in the ratio 3:2:1.

■ The proton resonance for the –CH_3 group occurs at the lowest chemical shift and that for the –OH group occurs at the highest. This is consistent with the greater shielding of the protons on the –CH_3 group compared with the de-shielding of the proton on the –OH group by the electronegative oxygen atom.

Type of proton	*Chemical shift/ppm*
R — CH_3	0.9
R — CH_2 — R	1.3
R_3CH	2.0
CH_3 — C(=O)OR	2.0
CH_3 — C(=O)R	2.1
⬡ — CH_3	2.3
R — C ≡ C — H	2.6
⬡ — CH(R)(R)	2.9
R — CH_2 — Hal	3.2–3.7
R — O — CH_3	3.8
R — O — H	4.5*
RHC = CH_2	4.9
RHC = CH_2	5.9
⬡ — OH	7.0*
⬡ — H	7.3
R — C(=O)H	9.7*
R — C(=O)OH	11.5*

● **Table 7.3** Typical proton chemical shift values (δ) relative to TMS = 0. Those marked by a star (*) are sensitive to solvent, substituents and concentration

Low-resolution n.m.r. spectroscopy is used in quality control laboratories on a routine basis *(figure 7.5)*. The instrument is designed and programmed for different applications. Solid and liquid samples are used, and a calibration procedure is included to provide quantitative results. For example, the oil content of seeds and the fat content of chocolate are found by proton n.m.r. Also, the small amounts of fluorine compounds that are added to toothpaste to increase the hardness of tooth enamel are accurately controlled with fluorine-19 (^{19}F) n.m.r.

SAQ 7.1

Explain why there are no peaks due to ^{12}C on the n.m.r. spectrum of ethanol.

SAQ 7.2

Using *table 7.3* sketch the low-resolution n.m.r. spectrum you would expect to obtain from

$$HO-\langle\bigcirc\rangle-CH_3$$

High-resolution n.m.r. spectra: spin–spin splitting

The n.m.r. spectrum of an organic compound does not always appear as a series of single peaks. Under very accurately controlled operating conditions, single peaks can be split or **resolved** into a number of parts *(figure 7.6)*. This is called high-resolution n.m.r. spectroscopy. The splitting of the peaks occurs because the spins of neighbouring protons interact or **couple** with one another. When

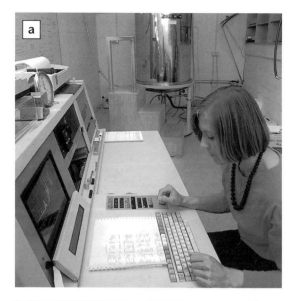

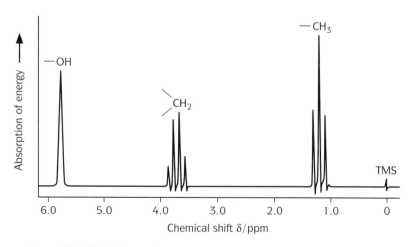

● *Figure 7.5* **a** A bench-top n.m.r. analyser. **b** Substances such as chocolate, seeds, polymers, oils, etc., are routinely analysed by n.m.r. spectroscopy.

● *Figure 7.6* The high-resolution n.m.r. spectrum of ethanol. Compare this with figure 7.4b.

the peak from a given proton is split, the extent of the splitting depends on the number of nuclei to which it is coupled.

Some rules concerning spin–spin splitting are as follows:

- Protons on the same atom (e.g. CH_3) do not interact with one another. They are equivalent and behave as a group.
- Protons on non-adjacent atoms (i.e. atoms that are *not* next to one another) are usually too far apart to interact with one another.
- A single peak will be split into ($n + 1$) parts by an adjacent group containing n equivalent protons.
- The splitting patterns arising from different numbers of protons, attached to the same atom, interacting with their neighbouring protons, are summarised in *figure 7.7*. This arrangement is called **Pascal's triangle**.

We can now compare the low-resolution and high-resolution spectra of ethanol, shown in *figures 7.4b* and *7.6*.

- The low-resolution CH_3 single peak is split into three parts on the high-resolution spectrum due to the protons on the adjacent CH_2 group.
- The low-resolution CH_2 single peak is split into four parts on the high-resolution spectrum due to the adjacent protons on the CH_3 group.
- Both of these splittings follow the ($n + 1$) rule.
- The low-resolution OH single peak does not

split under high resolution unless the ethanol is pure. This is because the protons attached to the oxygen atoms exchange rapidly with one another. They are called **labile** and experience only an *average* environment. Also, they do not interact with the protons on the neighbouring CH_2 group because of the short time for which they are attached to the molecule.

Worked examples

We can now suggest structures for unknown compounds using chemical shifts and spin–spin splitting patterns.

Figure 7.8a represents the n.m.r. spectrum of a ketone. It can be interpreted in the following way.

- Three peaks at $\delta = \sim 1$: due to the single peak from a CH_3 group split by the CH_2 group.
- One peak at $\delta = \sim 2$: due to the CH_3 group adjacent to C=O.
- Four peaks at $\delta = \sim 2$ to 3: due to the single peak from the CH_2 group split by the protons in the adjacent CH_3 group.
- The C=O group does not give a peak.

A possible structure is

$$CH_3 - \underset{\underset{O}{\|}}{C} - CH_2 - CH_3$$

butan-2-one

Figure 7.8b represents the n.m.r. spectrum of a substituted arene. Its interpretation is as follows.

- Two peaks at $\delta = \sim 1$: due to CH_3 group(s) split by a C–H group.
- Seven peaks at $\delta = \sim 3$: due to CH group(s) split by six adjacent protons, i.e. two methyl groups.

number of chemically equivalent protons causing splitting	splitting pattern with relative intensities											
1						1		1				
2					1		2		1			
3				1		3		3		1		
4			1		4		6		4		1	
5		1		5		10		10		5		1
6	1		6		15		20		15		6	1

● *Figure 7.7* Use of Pascal's triangle to determine splitting patterns.

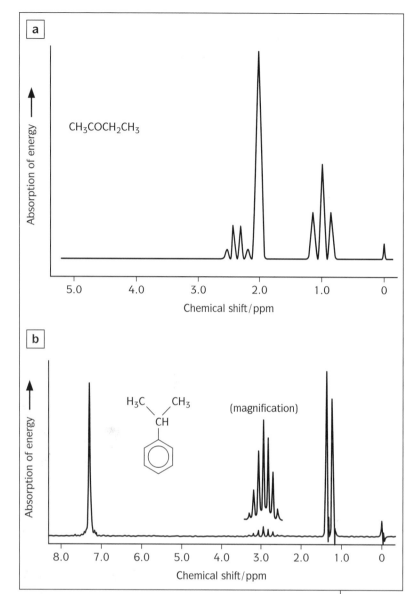

● *Figure 7.8* **a** The n.m.r. spectrum of a ketone. From an analysis of the peaks, it could be butan-2-one.
b The n.m.r. spectrum of a substituted arene. This could be 2-phenylpropane.

■ One peak at $\delta = \sim 7$: due to aromatic ring protons. Since these are not adjacent to the other proton groups, any interaction between them is too weak to cause splitting.

A possible structure for the compound is

2-phenylpropane

SAQ 7.3

Figure 7.9 shows the n.m.r. spectra of **a** an alkyl halide and **b** an aromatic acid. Suggest possible structures for these compounds.

Deuterium exchange in nuclear magnetic resonance

The deuterium nucleus (D = ^{2}H) with one proton and one neutron responds to n.m.r. at different frequencies to those needed for ^{1}H. This is useful in analysis for confirming the presence of a labile proton in groups such as OH, NH$_2$ and SH, which give single peaks.

For example, when deuterium oxide (D$_2$O, known as heavy water) is added to an alcohol, the following exchange reaction occurs:

$$ROH + DOD \rightleftharpoons ROD + HOD$$

The proton is no longer on the alcohol molecule, and the ROH peak disappears from its original position. A new peak in another position appears for HOD.

CDCl$_3$ is often used as a solvent instead of CHCl$_3$ in n.m.r. analysis to exclude unwanted signals from the spectrum.

Nuclear magnetic resonance in medical diagnosis

Magnetic resonance imaging (MRI) uses nuclear magnetic resonance to produce images of parts of the human body *(figure 7.10)*. You saw earlier (page 74) that, in the presence of an external magnetic field, atomic magnetic nuclei are aligned with or opposed to this field. The human body contains many types of magnetic nuclei, e.g. ^{1}H, ^{14}N, ^{31}P, etc. When part of the body is scanned with radiofrequency radiation in a magnetic field, some of these nuclei are reorientated and energy is released, which is related to the nuclear environment. This energy is

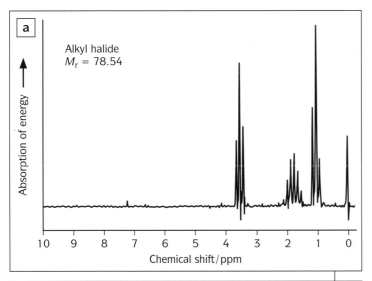

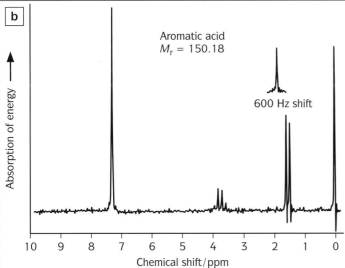

● **Figure 7.9** The n.m.r. spectra of **a** an alkyl halide and **b** an aromatic acid – but which compounds are they?

detected and the data are transformed by a computer into an image, which is used in clinical diagnosis for detecting abnormalities and diseased tissue *(figure 7.11)*.

The major use of MRI is in evaluating diseases of the brain and spine, but it has many other applications. Tumours are detected and treated. The nature of fats stored in the body and those circulating in the blood are studied to find the causes of heart disease. The metabolism of drugs and anaesthetics in the brain and liver can also be traced.

MRI has the advantages that it is non-invasive and the radiation is not harmful to the patients, in contrast to penetrating X-rays. It provides patients and doctors with a powerful means of investigation that was unheard-of a generation ago.

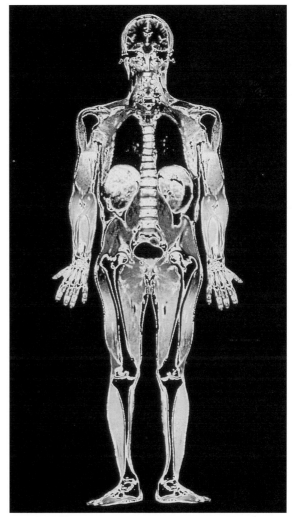

● **Figure 7.11** An MRI image of a human body.

● **Figure 7.10** An MRI machine in use.

SUMMARY

- N.m.r. spectroscopy is concerned with the absorption and emission of energy associated with the transition of nuclei between energy levels, in an external magnetic field.

- Nuclei consisting of an odd number of protons, or an odd number of neutrons, or both, possess spin, e.g. ^{1}H, and behave like tiny magnets, which can interact with electro-magnetic radiation to give a spectrum.

- When protons are placed in an external magnetic field, they become aligned either in a low-energy orientation in the same direction as the magnetic field or in a higher-energy orientation in opposition to the field.

- Low-energy radio waves are absorbed by some of the protons in the lower energy level. These protons change from being aligned with the external magnetic field to being opposed to it, and move to the higher level. At the same time, some of the protons in the higher energy level reverse their orientation and move to the lower energy level.

- The upwards and downwards transitions between the energy levels represent the resonance state. There is a net absorption of energy ΔE because there is a small excess of nuclei in the lower level.

- The sample (liquid, solid or solution) is placed in a constant external magnetic field and subjected to radio waves of varying frequency. When the frequency of the radiation exactly matches the energy difference between the two orientations $\Delta E = hf$, energy is absorbed and resonance occurs. The absorption of energy is plotted against the variation in frequency to give the n.m.r. spectrum.

- In chemical compounds, nuclei even of the same element give absorption peaks at slightly different frequencies owing to their different environments. These differences are known as chemical shifts and are measured relative to a standard, TMS.

- Chemical shifts have been recorded for protons in different environments and are used to identify chemical groups. Also, the area under each peak on the spectrum is proportional to the number of protons in a given environment.

- In low-resolution n.m.r. spectra, protons in a particular environment produce a single peak, which may be used simply for identification or quantitatively in quality control.

- In high-resolution n.m.r. spectra, the single peaks may be split because the nuclear spins of adjacent protons in molecules interact with one another. This is called spin–spin splitting. Predictable patterns of split peaks due to the specific arrangements of adjacent protons are obtained. From these patterns, possible structures for the molecules are deduced.

- Deuterium and D_2O are also used in n.m.r. analysis. The deuterium nucleus responds to the n.m.r. technique at different frequencies to those needed for ^{1}H, so the presence of a labile group in a molecule can be identified by replacing ^{1}H with D. When this is done, the ^{1}H absorption will disappear from the spectrum.

- N.m.r. is used in hospitals to produce magnetic resonance images of the human body. This technique is a powerful tool for investigating and treating diseases, particularly those of the brain and spine.

Questions

1 Sketch and explain the n.m.r. spectra you would expect from **a** benzene, **b** methylbenzene and **c** benzaldehyde.

2 Describe the information that may be obtained from proton n.m.r. spectra.

Combined techniques

1 explain the contribution that each of the spectra normally available for an unknown compound makes to a possible identification;

2 use evidence from up to three spectra to suggest a probable structure for a given compound;

3 suggest what further evidence might be required to confirm a structure suggested by a study of spectra.

Introduction

The spectroscopic techniques that you studied in earlier chapters are each limited in the type and amount of analytical data that it can provide. Atomic spectroscopy is useful for detecting and analysing metals. Infrared, ultraviolet/visible, nuclear magnetic resonance and mass spectro-scopies provide information on the chemical nature of compounds. In this chapter, we will explore how a combination of these techniques enables us to identify and to find the structure of organic compounds. With the exception of mass spectrometry, these methods are non-destructive, so all four spectra could be obtained with a small amount of sample.

When possible, the composition by mass of the elements is determined because this added infor-mation is helpful in identifying compounds. Carbon, hydrogen, nitrogen and sulphur can all be determined in a single operation by an elemental analyser *(figure 8.1)*. The sample is burned in oxygen and the gases formed (CO_2, H_2O, N_2 and SO_2) are separated by gas chromatography (chapter 1) and measured by thermal conductivity. Oxygen is determined separately by thermally decomposing the sample in the absence of added oxygen. (This technique is called **pyrolysis**.) The oxygen in the compound is measured as carbon monoxide. Halogens are measured as HX.

Identification and structure determination

The contribution that each type of spectrum can make to our knowledge of a compound is summarised in *table 8.1*.

Type of spectrum	Information provided on the nature of the compound
Mass	Accurate molecular mass from the molecular-ion peak. Possible structure from the fragmentation pattern. The number of carbon atoms present from the [M + 1] molecular-ion peak. The presence of halogens from the [M + 2] and [M + 4] molecular-ion peaks
Infrared	The presence of functional groups from the wavenumbers of the absorption bands. The identity of the compound using the 'fingerprint' region
Ultraviolet/ visible	The identity of unsaturated groups, e.g. chromophores, from the wavelengths of the absorption bands. The extent of unsaturation in a molecule, e.g. conjugation, from alterations in the characteristic absorption wavelengths. Possible structure from the absorption bands
Nuclear magnetic resonance	The identity of chemical groups containing protons from chemical shift. The arrangement of proton-containing groups in the molecule from the spin–spin splitting pattern.

● **Table 8.1** Identity and structural data from different spectra.

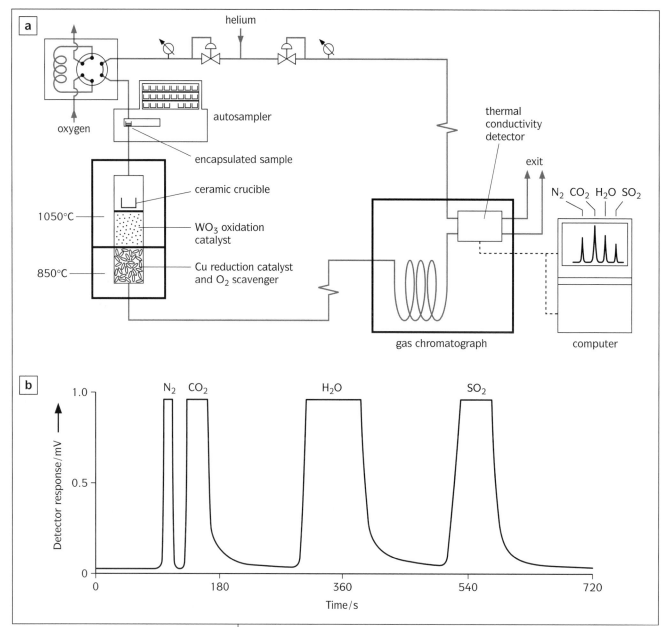

● *Figure 8.1* **a** Diagram of an elemental analyser. This is used to find the percentage amounts by mass of carbon, hydrogen, nitrogen and sulphur in a compound.
b A gas chromatographic trace from an elemental analyser, showing the separation of the combustion products. The area of each peak is proportional to the mass of each product.

It is not always necessary to record and interpret all four spectra to identify and to suggest a structure for an unknown compound. Ultraviolet/visible spectra are usually the least helpful. The intensities of the absorption bands are an important feature of these spectra as they depend on the structures of the compounds. Compounds are listed in databases according to the intensity of their strongest band. But these bands are broad, the spectra are simple and it is often difficult to distinguish between structurally related compounds. They are, however, useful for confirming deductions from the other types of spectra.

In infrared spectra the O–H stretching absorption bands are also broad because of the hydrogen bonding. They will only appear as sharp peaks if the sample is in dilute solution or in the vapour phase.

Worked examples

Compound A (figure 8.2)

The i.r. spectrum indicates that the compound is relatively simple. The sharp absorption band at $\sim 3000\,cm^{-1}$ indicates a C–H bond, and the band at $\sim 1200\,cm^{-1}$ could be due to the presence of a C–O bond.

The n.m.r. spectrum suggests the presence of two equivalent –CH$_3$ groups splitting the single peak of a –CH group into seven parts. The single peak of the –CH$_3$ groups is split into two parts by the –CH group.

The mass spectrum shows an M$^+$ and an [M + 2]$^+$ peak at *m/e* 122 and 124, suggesting the presence of a halogen. The [M + 1]$^+$ and [M + 3]$^+$ peaks are approximately 3.3% of their corresponding M$^+$ peaks, indicating that there are three carbon atoms in the molecule. The group of peaks at *m/e* 41 to 43 are due to the hydrocarbon part of the molecule without the halogen ^{79}Br and ^{81}Br, i.e. M$^+$ − bromine.

The compound is

$$CH_3 - CH - CH_3$$
$$|$$
$$Br$$

2-bromopropane

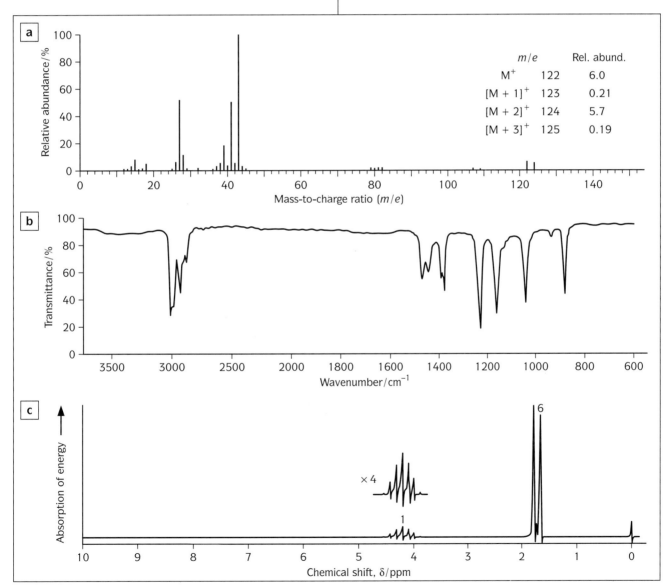

● **Figure 8.2** Compound A: **a** the mass spectrum, **b** the i.r. spectrum (liquid film), and **c** the n.m.r. spectrum (in CCl$_4$).

Compound B (figure 8.3)

The i.r. spectrum shows an absorption band at ~1700 cm^{-1}, which indicates the presence of a C=O bond. The broad band at 2500 to 3300 cm^{-1} indicates the presence of an –OH group in an acid.

The composition by mass of the elements is useful at this stage. You saw in *Foundation Chemistry* (chapter 2) how the empirical formula of a compound is calculated from this information. The empirical formula is worked out in *table 8.2*.

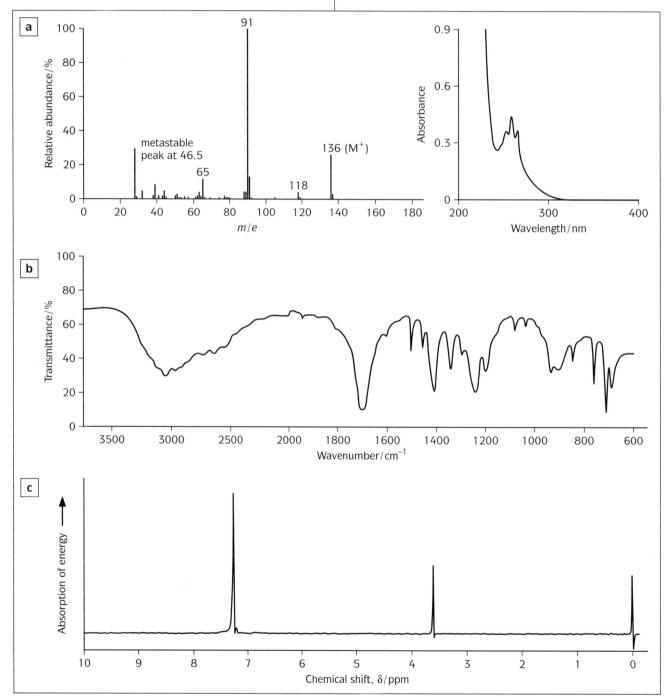

● *Figure 8.3* Compound B: **a** the mass spectrum, **b** the i.r. spectrum (KBr disc) and **c** the n.m.r. spectrum. Also shown as an inset in (**a**) is the u.v. spectrum of 12 mg of B in 50 cm^3 of 95% C$_2$H$_5$OH. Elemental analysis of compound B gave the composition by mass of the elements: C, 70.7%; H, 6.0%; O, 23.3%.

	C	*H*	*O*
percentage by mass	70.7	6.0	23.3
amount/mol	$\dfrac{70.7}{12} = 5.89$	$\dfrac{6.0}{1} = 6$	$\dfrac{23.3}{16} = 1.46$
Divide by the smallest to give whole numbers of atoms per molecule =	4	4	1

● *Table 8.2*

The empirical formula is therefore C_4H_4O, and the empirical molecular mass is $M_r = 68$.

The mass spectrum shows that $M^+ = 136$. Therefore, the molecular formula is $C_8H_8O_2$.

Molecules that could fit these data are

$C_6H_5CH_2COOH$

or one of the forms of

CH_3—⬡—COOH   (i.e. 1,2-, 1,3- or 1,4-)

The mass spectrum also shows a large peak at *m/e* 91, but this could represent the fragment ions $[C_6H_5CH_2]^+$ or

$$\left[CH_3-C\underset{\underset{H}{C-C}}{\overset{\overset{H}{C-C}}{\bigcirc}}C- \right]^+$$

The n.m.r. spectrum shows a single peak at $\delta = {\sim}7$, which indicates a phenyl group, and the single peak at $\delta = 3$ to 4 suggests the presence of a CH_2 group. Neither of these peaks is split because the proton groups are not adjacent.

If CH_3—⬡ were present in the molecule, a peak would be expected at $\delta = {\sim}2.3$.

The compound is

$C_6H_5CH_2COOH$
phenylethanoic acid

The u.v. absorption band with a maximum at ~260 nm is consistent with the strongest absorption band for molecules of this structural type.

Confirmation of a structure

You can see from these examples that, while all the spectra contribute in some way to the analysis of the compound, the evidence from just one or two techniques can hold the key to solving the problem. In the analysis of compound A, the mass spectrum made the essential contribution; whereas with compound B, the final choice of structure was based on the evidence from the n.m.r. spectrum.

In many cases, it is important to recognise what further evidence is required to confirm the structure of a compound. For example, in the analysis of a hydrocarbon that has two isomers, the infrared spectrum only shows absorptions due to C–H bonds. The mass spectrum gives the relative molecular mass and the number of carbon atoms, and the fragmentation pattern may indicate the most likely structure. But to confirm this structure, an n.m.r. spectrum is required (*figure 8.4*).

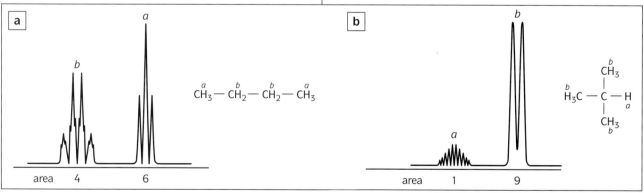

● *Figure 8.4* Structures and n.m.r. spectra of the two isomers of the hydrocarbon, butane
C_4H_{10}: **a** butane (old name n-butane) and **b** 2-methylpropane (old name isobutane).
The groups of peaks due to the protons in different environments are labelled *a* and *b*.

SAQ 8.1

Suggest, with reasons, which spectroscopic techniques would be essential to identify and to find the structures of the following compounds:

a $CH_3CHClCH_3$

b $CH_3CH_2CH_2COOH$

c CH_3COOCH_3

d HO—⟨benzene ring⟩—C\(\overset{O}{\underset{H}{\parallel}}\)

SUMMARY

■ I.r., u.v./visible, n.m.r. and mass spectra are all used in the analysis of organic compounds. Frequently, it is not possible to establish an identity or structure from one technique alone.

■ The compounds are most quickly and easily analysed by combining the four techniques. This is because the information provided by one spectrum may fill the gaps in information from another. The various spectra complement one another.

■ The method involves recognising the important features of each spectrum and fitting the information together like the pieces of a jigsaw puzzle.

■ A satisfactory analysis can often be completed with only three spectra, providing there is enough evidence to confirm the identity and structure.

Questions

The following questions and spectra for different types of compounds are provided for you to gain experience of analysis by combined spectroscopic techniques.

1 Identify compound P from the spectra in *figure 8.5*.

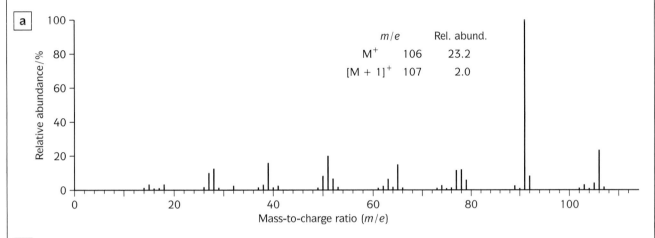

	m/e	Rel. abund.
M⁺	106	23.2
[M + 1]⁺	107	2.0

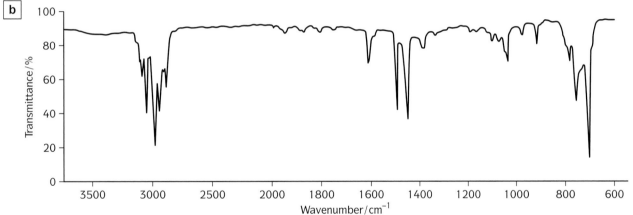

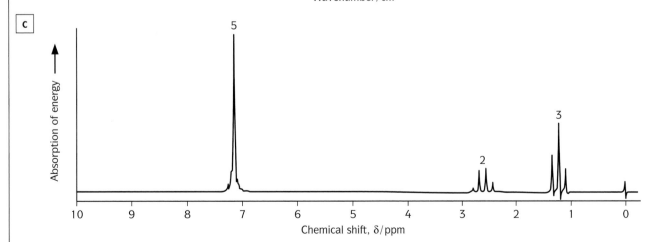

● *Figure 8.5* Compound P: **a** the mass spectrum, **b** the i.r. spectrum and **c** the n.m.r. spectrum.

Questions

2 Identify compound Q from the spectra in *figure 8.6*.

a

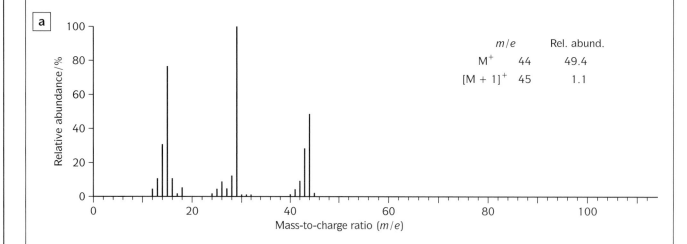

	m/e	Rel. abund.
M$^+$	44	49.4
[M + 1]$^+$	45	1.1

b

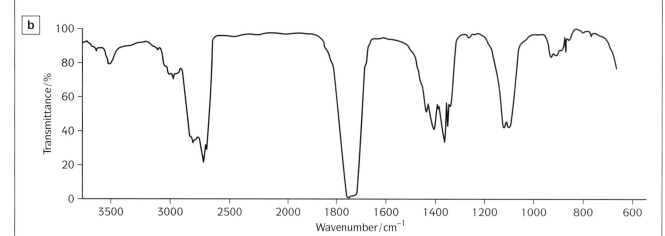

c

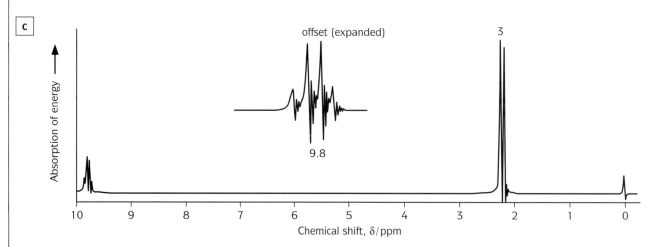

● *Figure 8.6* Compound Q: **a** the mass spectrum, **b** the i.r. spectrum and **c** the n.m.r. spectrum.

Questions

3 Identify compound R from the spectra in *figure 8.7*.

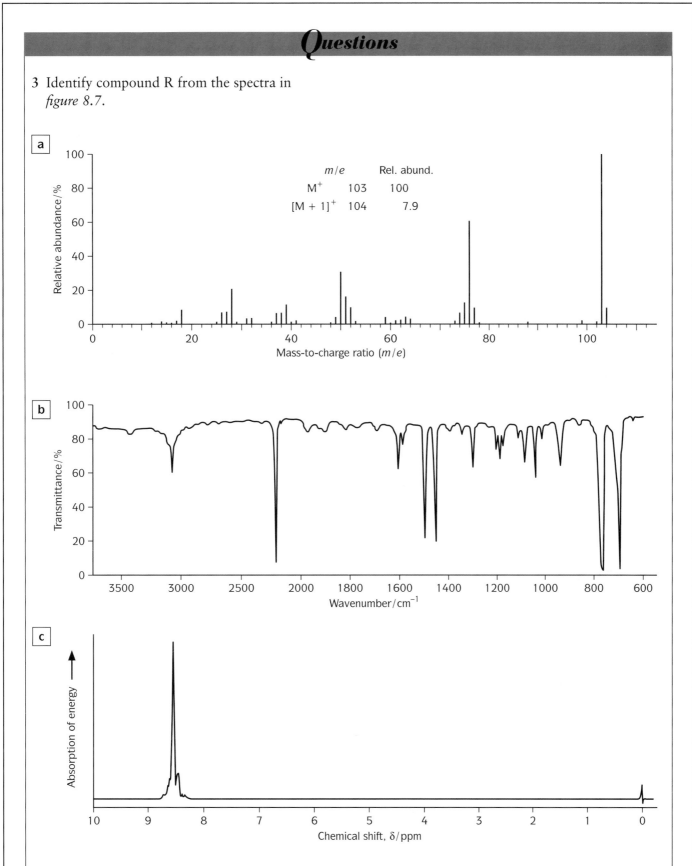

	m/e	Rel. abund.
M^+	103	100
$[M + 1]^+$	104	7.9

● *Figure 8.7* Compound R: **a** the mass spectrum, **b** the i.r. spectrum and **c** the n.m.r. spectrum.

Questions

4 Identify compound S from the spectra in *figure 8.8.*

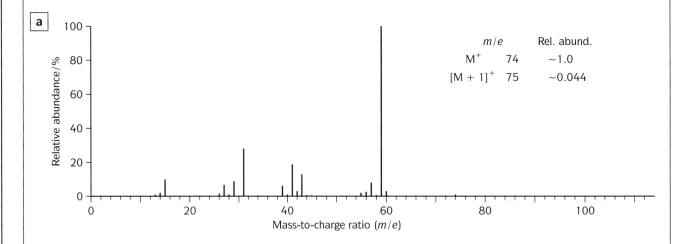

	m/e	Rel. abund.
M⁺	74	~1.0
[M + 1]⁺	75	~0.044

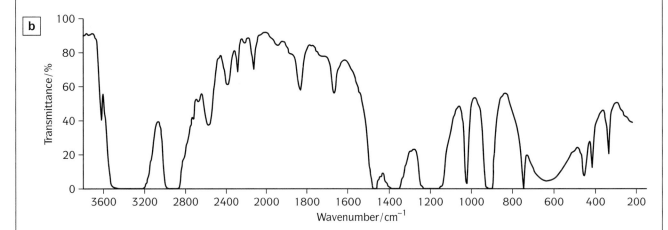

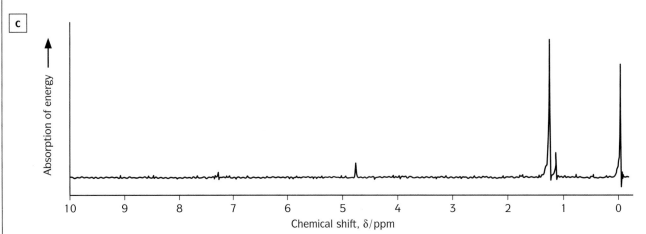

● **Figure 8.8** Compound S: **a** the mass spectrum, **b** the i.r. spectrum and **c** the n.m.r. spectrum.

Questions

5 Identify compound T from the spectra in *figure 8.9*.

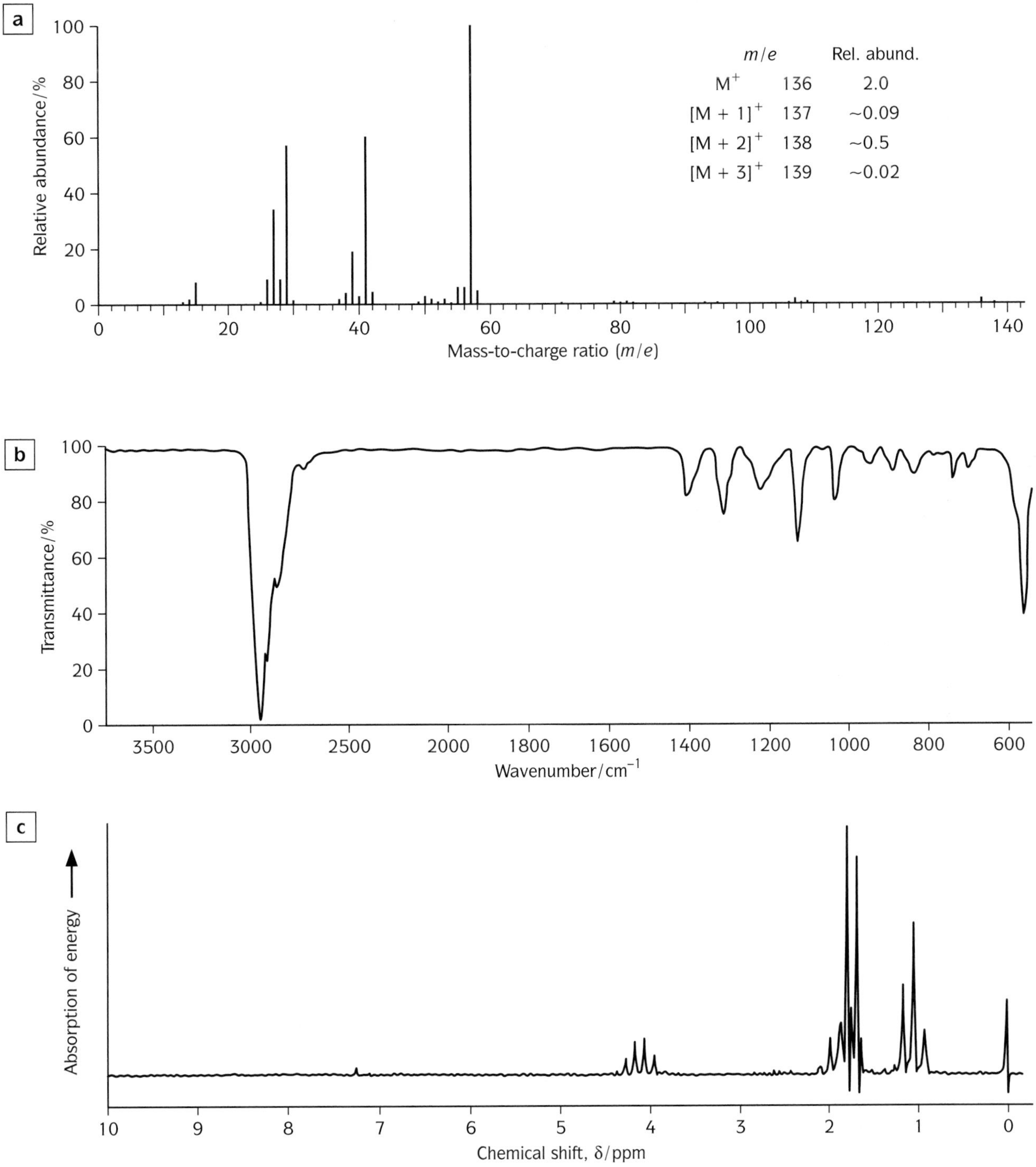

a

	m/e	Rel. abund.
M$^+$	136	2.0
[M + 1]$^+$	137	~0.09
[M + 2]$^+$	138	~0.5
[M + 3]$^+$	139	~0.02

b

c

● *Figure 8.9* Compound T: **a** the mass spectrum, **b** the i.r. spectrum and **c** the n.m.r. spectrum.

Questions

6 Identify compound U from the spectra in
figure 8.10.

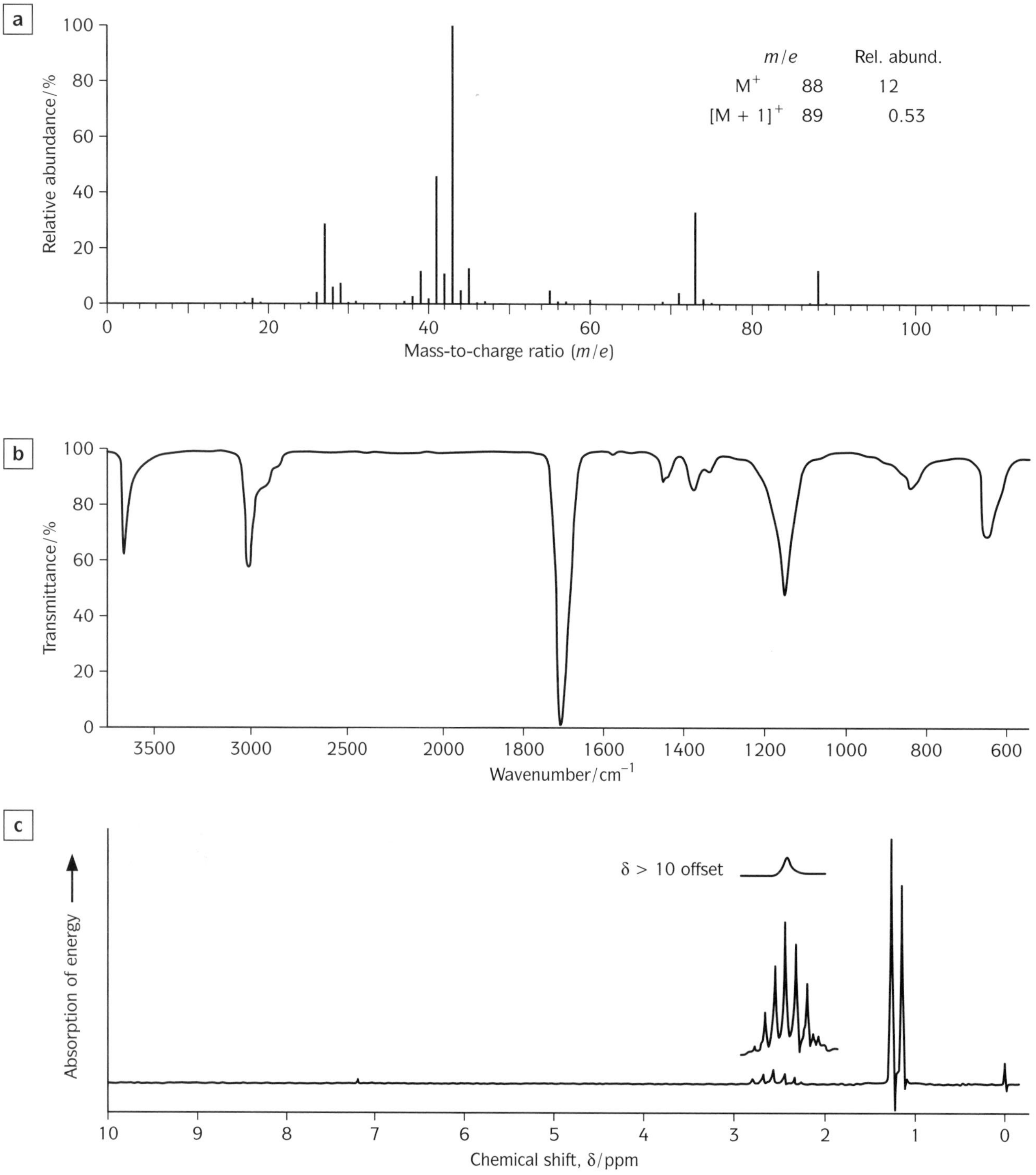

a

	m/e	Rel. abund.
M⁺	88	12
[M + 1]⁺	89	0.53

b

c

δ > 10 offset

● *Figure 8.10* Compound U: **a** the mass spectrum, **b** the i.r. spectrum and
c the n.m.r. spectrum.

Answers to self-assessment questions

Chapter 1

1.1 Any two of the following:

(i) Thin-layer chromatography is faster than paper chromatography.

(ii) The thin layer may be made from different solids. So a wide variety of mixtures can be separated by careful choice of the mobile and stationary phases.

(iii) Thin-layer chromatography can be used for quickly selecting the best conditions for larger-scale separations.

1.2 Compound 1 $R_f = \dfrac{1.5}{12.5} = 0.12$

Compound 2 $R_f = \dfrac{9.1}{12.5} = 0.73$

Compound 1 has a greater affinity for the thin layer than compound 2.

1.3 **a** By measuring the difference in time between the injection of the sample and the centre of the peak for a component.

b The areas under the peaks represent the amounts of the components in the mixture.

1.4 **a** Paper chromatography or thin-layer chromatography.

b Gas/liquid chromatography.

c High-performance liquid chromatography or thin-layer chromatography.

1.5 **a** A methanol CH_3OH

B ethanol C_2H_5OH

C butan-1-ol $CH_3CH_2CH_2CH_2OH$

D 2-methylbutan-1-ol

$$CH_3-CH_2-\overset{\overset{\displaystyle CH_3}{|}}{\underset{\underset{\displaystyle OH}{|}}{C}}-CH_3$$

b Peaks   A : B : C : D

Relative amounts 1 : 10 : 2 : 2

1.6 Charge, shape and size.

1.7 **a**

$$\overset{+}{H_3N}-\overset{\overset{\displaystyle CH_3}{|}}{CH}-COO^-$$

b The COO^- group becomes protonated:

$$\overset{+}{H_3N}-\overset{\overset{\displaystyle CH_3}{|}}{CH}-COO^- \;+\; H^+ \longrightarrow \overset{+}{H_3N}-\overset{\overset{\displaystyle CH_3}{|}}{CH}-COOH$$

1.8 Electrophoresis is used to separate the small fragments of DNA on a gel. This method separates the fragments according to their charge and size without altering them in any way.

Chapter 2

2.1 42.0468 propene $CH_3-CH=CH_2$

44.0261 ethanal $CH_3-\overset{\overset{\displaystyle \;}{\underset{\underset{\displaystyle O}{\|}}{C}}}-H$

2.2 **a**

Peak	m/e	Ion
D	58	M^+ $[CH_3CH_2CH_2CH_3]^+$
C	43	fragment $[CH_3CH_2CH_2]^+$
B	29	fragment $[CH_3CH_2]^+$
A	15	fragment $[CH_3]^+$

b For example

$$[CH_3CH_2CH_2CH_3]^+ \longrightarrow [CH_3CH_2CH_2]^+ + CH_3\cdot$$

2.3 When the molecular ion fragments into smaller pieces, see *Table 2.2*, the CH_3 group (m/e 15) may be neutral while the larger fragment carries the charge.

2.4 There are two isotopes of chlorine. The three peaks represents three types of Cl_2^+ molecule.

m/e 70   represents $^{35}Cl-^{35}Cl$

m/e 72   represents $^{35}Cl-^{37}Cl$

m/e 74   represents $^{37}Cl-^{37}Cl$

If the sample contains one molecule of $^{37}Cl-^{37}Cl$, there will be six molecules of $^{35}Cl-^{37}Cl$ and nine molecules of $^{35}Cl-^{35}Cl$. So ^{35}Cl is the most abundant isotope. The isotopes are present in the ratio of 24 atoms of ^{35}Cl to eight atoms of ^{37}Cl, i.e. 3:1.

The relative atomic mass of chlorine in the sample is therefore

$$A_r = \frac{(3 \times 35) + (1 \times 37)}{4} = 35.5$$

2.5 There are two isotopes of bromine, ^{79}Br and ^{81}Br. Possible combinations in CH_2Br_2 are: $^{79}Br-^{79}Br$, $^{79}Br-^{81}Br$, $^{81}Br-^{81}Br$. There will be three peaks.

m/e	*Ion*
172	$[CH_2\,^{79}Br\,^{79}Br]^+$
174	$[CH_2\,^{79}Br\,^{81}Br]^+$
176	$[CH_2\,^{81}Br\,^{81}Br]^+$

2.6 **a** M^+ $[CH_3CH_2COOH]^+$, *m/e* = 74

b *m/e* 15, $[CH_3]^+$
$[CH_3CH_2COOH]^+$
$\longrightarrow [CH_3]^+ + CH_2COOH\cdot$

m/e 29, $[CH_3CH_2]^+$
$[CH_3CH_2COOH]^+$
$\longrightarrow [CH_3CH_2]^+ + COOH\cdot$

m/e 45, $[COOH]^+$
$[CH_3CH_2COOH]^+$
$\longrightarrow [COOH]^+ + CH_3CH_2\cdot$

m/e 73, $[CH_3CH_2COO]^+$
$[CH_3CH_2COOH]^+$
$\longrightarrow [CH_3CH_2COO]^+ + H\cdot$

c

$$\begin{array}{c} \quad\; H \;\; H \\ \quad\; | \;\;\; | \qquad\;\; O \\ H - C - C - C \diagup\!\!\diagdown \\ \quad\; | \;\;\; | \qquad\; OH \\ \quad\; H \;\; H \end{array}$$

Chapter 3

3.1 $f = \dfrac{3.00 \times 10^8\,ms^{-1}}{450 \times 10^{-9}\,m} = 6.67 \times 10^{14}\,s^{-1}$

3.2 $\Delta E = hf = \dfrac{hc}{\lambda}$

So $\Delta E = \dfrac{6.63 \times 10^{-34}\,Js \times 3.00 \times 10^8\,ms^{-1}}{200 \times 10^{-9}\,m}$

$= 9.945 \times 10^{-19}\,J$ per molecule

or $\Delta E = \dfrac{9.945 \times 10^{-19}\,J \times 6.02 \times 10^{23}\,mol^{-1}}{1000}$

$= 598.69\,kJ\,mol^{-1}$

3.3 Rutherford proposed that the atom consisted of a positive nucleus containing most of the mass of the atom surrounded by negatively charged electrons.

Bohr proposed that these electrons surrounding the nucleus exist in orbits of certain energy levels where they are stable.

3.4 It has the simplest electronic structure – only one electron.

3.5 No. The Balmer series is formed by electrons falling back to the second energy level $n = 2$, whereas the ionisation energy is the amount of energy required to remove the electron from the ground state, i.e. from $n = 1$ level.

3.6 $\Delta E = hf = \dfrac{hc}{\lambda}$

$= \dfrac{6.63 \times 10^{-34}\,Js \times 3.00 \times 10^8\,ms^{-1}}{589 \times 10^{-9}\,m}$

$= 3.38 \times 10^{-19}\,J$

3.7 **a** Antibonding molecular orbitals are at a higher energy level than bonding molecular orbitals.

b There must be an empty space (a vacancy) in the 3d orbitals of the complex metal ion so that, when they are split into two energy levels, an electron can move up to the higher level.

Chapter 4

4.1 Mercury

4.2 Very much smaller samples can be analysed. The analysis can be done more quickly.

4.3 Flame temperature control is more important in atomic emission spectroscopy. This is because the intensities of the emitted spectral lines are more sensitive to temperature variation than those of the atomic absorption lines.

4.4 A lower-temperature flame is used to prevent the excitation of other metals. This gives a simple spectrum, and the required lines from sodium and potassium are isolated by filters. Also, lithium may be used as an internal standard, and this gives more accurate results.

Chapter 5

5.1 The wavelength absorbed at 490 nm is the blue-green radiation of the visible part of the spectrum. The complementary colour transmitted is red.

5.2 When the complex with ammonia is formed, the energy difference ΔE between the d−d orbitals is increased and radiation of shorter wavelength is absorbed.

5.3

	Chromophores	Transitions
$C_6H_5COCH_3$	C_6H_5	$\pi \longrightarrow \pi^*$
	$>C=O$	$\pi \longrightarrow \pi^*$ and $n \longrightarrow \pi^*$
$CH_3CH=CHCHO$	$>C=C$	$\pi \longrightarrow \pi^*$
	$>C=O$	$\pi \longrightarrow \pi^*$ and $n \longrightarrow \pi^*$

5.4

	C	H	N
percentage by mass	67.9	5.7	26.4
amount/mol	$\frac{67.9}{12} = 5.66$	$\frac{5.7}{1} = 5.7$	$\frac{26.4}{14} = 1.89$
divide by the smallest to give whole numbers of atoms per molecule	3	3	1

$\lambda_{max} = 160$ nm indicates $-C\equiv N$

$\lambda_{max} = 190$ nm indicates $>C=C$

The structure could be

$$\begin{array}{cc} H & H \\ | & | \\ C=C & -C\equiv N \\ | \\ H \end{array}$$

5.5 The electrons in the π and π^* orbitals of each chromophore interact with those of another and become delocalised. They form new orbitals in which the highest-energy π orbital and the lowest-energy π^* orbital are closer together in energy. Since the energy difference is less, a longer wavelength is absorbed.

5.6 The solutions must be dilute.

5.7 a For violet and purple solutions, use yellow-green and green filters.

b For blue and green solutions, use orange and purple filters.

Chapter 6

6.1 Oxygen is more electronegative than carbon and attracts the electrons from the carbon atom.

6.2 a See *figure*.

Linear structure

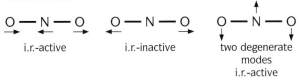

Angular structure

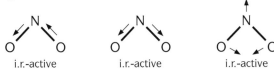

b Nitrogen dioxide has an angular structure or symmetry.

6.3 2500−3300 cm^{-1} O−H hydrogen bonded in acids

2840−3095 cm^{-1} C−H

1680−1750 cm^{-1} C=O

1610−1680 cm^{-1} C=C

An aromatic carboxylic acid.

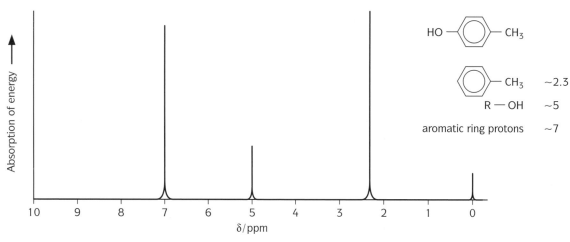

● **Answer for** SAQ 7.2

Chapter 7

7.1 Carbon-12 does not contain an odd number of protons or an odd number of neutrons and so does not have a nuclear spin.

7.2 See *figure*.

7.3 **a** 1-Chloropropane $CH_3CH_2CH_2Cl$

b 2-Phenylpropanoic acid

Chapter 8

8.1 **a** $CH_3CHClCH_3$

(i) Mass spectrometry to find M_r from the M^+ peak, to detect the presence of the halogen atom from the M^+ and $[M + 2]^+$ peaks, to find the number of carbon atoms in the molecule from the $[M + 1]^+$ and $[M + 3]^+$ peaks, and to find a possible structure for the molecule from the fragmentation pattern.

(ii) N.m.r. to identify the chemical groups that contain protons, from their chemical shifts, and to find their arrangement in the molecule from the spin–spin splitting pattern.

b $CH_3CH_2CH_2COOH$

(i) Mass spectrometry to find M_r from the M^+ peak, the number of carbon atoms in the molecule and a possible structure for the molecule.

(ii) I.r. to identify the functional groups C=O and O–H in the acid. Or use n.m.r.

c CH_3COOCH_3

(i) Mass spectrometry to find M_r, the number of carbon atoms in the molecule and a possible structure.

(ii) I.r. to identify the C=O group in the ester. Or use n.m.r.

d

(i) Mass spectrometry to find M_r, the number of carbon atoms in the molecule and a possible structure.

(ii) N.m.r. to identify the chemical groups containing protons and find their arrangement in the molecule.

Index (Numbers in italics refer to figures.)